A COMPLETE GUIDE TO MAKING TASTY AND ORIGINAL PANINI FOR ANY OCCASION

(100 + RECIPES)

SIMPLE STEP-BY-STEP GUIDE TO MAKING DELICIOUS, TASTY AND EASY PANINI TO CREATE

By

Ada ROSSI

TABLE OF CONTENS

INTRODUCTION

A panino is a sandwich made from crusty Italian bread (such as ciabatta, and michetta), usually served warmed by grilling or taosting. An example of the types of bread used for sandwiches is bargiglio, focaccia and focaccia. The bread is cut inside and stuffed with fresh ingredients, such as ham, blueberry, prosciutto, milk, or other foods, and then the bread is pressed with a steam grill. Panini is a word from the Italian origin. In Italian, noun panino (Italian plural panini) is a diminutive of bread ("pane") and refers to a sandwich. Panino imbottito ("stuffed panino") refers to a sandwich, but the word panino is also often used alone to indicate a sandwich in general. Similar to the sandwich is the tramezzino, a trangular or square sandwich consisting of two slices of soft white bread without a crust. In English-speaking countries, panini is widely used as singular form, with the form plural panini or paninis, although some speakers use singular panino and plural panini as in Italian. The term "Panino" became a symbol of a youth culture, characterised by sandwich shops such as "Al Panino in Milan" and "American fast forst". Panini have been conceived as a trendy product, fused with the environment and clothing, and have struggled to show off the Panino has become a status symbol since the 1980s. In this book. With this book you will have a step-by-step guide to making delicious, tasty and original Panini suitable for any occasion: at home for snacks, lunch or dinner or to take with you on trips or weekends in the countryside or at the seaside. You can't do without this vademecum which will follow you precisely to make "perfect panini".

1. SLICES BREAD AND BANANA PANINI

Servings: 4   Prep Time:10 Minutes   Cook Time: 10 Minutes

INGREDIENTS

- ✓ 2 slices bread
- ✓ 1 banana slices
- ✓ 2 oz. chocolate

DIRECTIONS

- ➢ Melt the butter in a frying pan over medium heat.
- ➢ Add the apple slices and thyme.
- ➢ Cook for 4 minutes. Remove from the heat and leave to cool.
- ➢ Preheat the Panini press.
- ➢ Coat each slice of bread with mustard.
- ➢ Sprinkle 1/4 cup cheese on 4 slices of bread.
- ➢ Top each with 2 slices of ham.
- ➢ Add apple mixture on top of ham
- ➢ Sprinkle with remaining cheese.
- ➢ Cover with remaining bread slices.
- ➢ Place 2 sandwiches on a hot Panini press.
- ➢ Close the Panini press and
- ➢ Bake for 5-6 minutes or until golden brown.
- ➢ Serve and enjoy

2. APPLE HAM CHEESE PANINI

Servings: 4   Prep Time:10 Minutes   Cook Time: 10 Minutes

INGREDIENTS:

- ✓ 8 bread slices
- ✓ 8 ham slices
- ✓ 2 cups Gruyere cheese, shredded
- ✓ 1/2 cup whole-grain mustard
- ✓ 1 tbsp thyme, chopped
- ✓ 2 apples, peel, cored, & sliced thinly
- ✓ 2 tbsp butter, melted

DIRECTIONS:

- ➢ Melt the butter in a frying pan over medium heat.
- ➢ Add the apple slices and thyme.
- ➢ Cook for 4 minutes. Remove from the heat and leave to cool.
- ➢ Preheat the Panini press.
- ➢ Coat each slice of bread with mustard.
- ➢ Sprinkle 1/4 cup cheese on 4 slices of bread.
- ➢ Top each with 2 slices of ham.
- ➢ Add apple mixture on top of ham
- ➢ Sprinkle with remaining cheese.
- ➢ Cover with remaining bread slices.
- ➢ Place 2 sandwiches on a hot Panini press.
- ➢ Close the Panini press and
- ➢ Bake for 5-6 minutes or until golden brown.
- ➢ Serve and enjoy

3. STRAWBERRY PANINI

Servings: 4   Prep.Time:10 Minutes   Cook Time: 10 Minutes

INGREDIENTS
- ✓ 2 slices bread
- ✓ 1 banana sliced
- ✓ 2 oz. strawberry

DIRECTIONS
- ➢ Prepare the bread for the sandwiches
- ➢ Place all the ingredients on one slice of bread
- ➢ Cover with the other slice of bread
- ➢ Toast the sandwich until golden brown
- ➢ Serve when ready

4. TOMATO CHEDDAR PANINI

Servings: 2   Prep Time:10 Minutes   Cook Time: 5 Minutes

INGREDIENTS:
- ✓ 4 bread slices
- ✓ 1 tbsp butter
- ✓ 1 tomato, sliced
- ✓ 4 Colby jack cheese slices
- ✓ 1 tsp lemon juice
- ✓ 1 avocado, mashed
- ✓ 1/2 tsp salt

DIRECTIONS:
- ➢ In a small bowl, mix avocado, lemon juice and salt.
- ➢ Preheat the Panini press.
- ➢ Spread butter on one side of each slice of bread.
- ➢ Take 2 slices of bread and spread them with the avocado mixture, then cover with the tomato and cheese.
- ➢ Cover with the other slices of bread. Make sure the buttered side is on top.
- ➢ Place the sandwiches on a hot panini press. Close the panini press and bake for 4-5 minutes or until golden brown.
- ➢ Serve and enjoy.

5. PINEAPPLE PANINI

Servings: 2 Minutes   Prep Time:5 minutes   Cook Time: 5 minute

INGREDIENTS
- ✓ 2 slices bread
- ✓ 2 oz. strawberry
- ✓ 2 oz. pineapple

DIRECTIONS:
- ➢ Prepare bread for the panini
- ➢ Place all the ingredients on a bread slice
- ➢ Top with the other bread slice
- ➢ Toast panini until golden brown Serve when ready

6. .ROAST BEEF & PEPPERS PANINI

Servings:4   **Cook. Time:1 5 Minutes**   **Prep.Time: 45 Minute**

INGREDIENTS
- ✓ 10 slices rye bread
- ✓ 15 slices deli roast beef
- ✓ 1 red bell pepper
- ✓ 10 slices baby Swiss cheese
- ✓ 2 tablespoons basil
- ✓ 5 tablespoons mayonnaise
- ✓ 1 green bell pepper
- ✓ 1 yellow bell pepper
- ✓ 1⁄3 cup olive oil

DIRECTIONS
- ➢ Julienne each of the peppers into thin slices.
- ➢ Place in a baking tray
- ➢ Then roast the peppers under an open grill
- ➢ Wait until the skin begins to brown approx.
- ➢ Cook about 5 - 10 minutes
- ➢ Remove from the grill and leave to cool.
- ➢ Spread a thin layer of mayo
- ➢ Place the mayo inside each slice of rye bread
- ➢ Mix the olive oil and basil in a small dish.
- ➢ Brush opposite side of 5 slices of bread
- ➢ Use the olive oil and basil mixture to brush.
- ➢ Place the 5 slices of bread on a preheated plate.
- ➢ The olive oil must be on the underside.
- ➢ Take 3 slices of roast beef
- ➢ Place the meat on top of each slice of bread
- ➢ Place the roasted peppers on top of the beef.
- ➢ Add 2 slices of Swiss baby cheese.
- ➢ Take 5 more slices of rye bread.
- ➢ Place the cheese on top with the mayonnaise facing down.
- ➢ Cut each sandwich in half for serving
- ➢ Brush the tops with the olive oil and basil mixture.
- ➢ Grill until the cheese is melted
- ➢ Then wait until the sandwich is golden brown on both sides

7. ROAST BEEF APPLE CHEESE PANINI

Servings:4   **Cook. Time:10 Minutes**   **Prep.Time: 10 Minute**

INGREDIENTS:
- ✓ 8 bread slices
- ✓ 1 apple, thinly sliced
- ✓ 6 oz cheddar cheese, sliced
- ✓ 12 oz leftover roast beef, sliced
- ✓ 2 tbsp butter
- ✓ 2 tbsp horseradish
- ✓ 3/4 cup mayonnaise

DIRECTIONS:
- ➢ In a small bowl, mix the mayonnaise and horseradish.
- ➢ Preheat the Panini press.
- ➢ Spread butter on one side of each slice of bread.
- ➢ Take 4 slices of bread and spread with mayonnaise.
- ➢ Mix and top with beef, apple, cheese.
- ➢ Cover with the remaining bread slices.
- ➢ Make sure the buttered side is on top.
- ➢ Place 2 sandwiches on a hot Panini press.
- ➢ Close panini press.
- ➢ Bake for 5 minutes or until golden brown.
- ➢ Serve and enjoy

8. ROAST BEEF PESTO PANINI

Servings:4 **Cook. Time:10 Minutes** **Prep.Time: 15 Minute**

INGREDIENTS

- ✓ 8 slices Italian bread, about 1/2 in thick
- ✓ 2 tablespoons butter, softened
- ✓ 4 tablespoons prepared basil pesto
- ✓ Spaghetti sauce, if desired for dipping
- ✓ 1/2 lb deli roast beef, cooked, thinly sliced
- ✓ 4 slices mozzarella cheese

DIRECTIONS

- ➤ Spread 1 side of each slice of bread with butter.
- ➤ Place 4 slices of bread with the butter side down on a 12-inch pan.
- ➤ Top the bread with the beef, pesto and cheese.
- ➤ Top with the remaining slice of bread with the butter side up.
- ➤ Cook the sandwiches in a frying pan or grill over medium heat for 4-5 minutes.
- ➤ Turn the sandwiches until crispy.
- ➤ Check that the cheese has melted.
- ➤ Serve with spaghetti sauce, if desired.

9. TOMATO ONION ROAST BEEF PANINI

Servings:4 **Cooking Time: 10 Minutes** **Prep.Time: 10 Minutes**

INGREDIENTS:

- ✓ 8 bread slices
- ✓ 1 onion, sliced
- ✓ 2 tomatoes, sliced
- ✓ 2 tbsp butter
- ✓ 8 provolone cheese slices
- ✓ 1 lb deli roast beef slices
- ✓ 1/4 cup mayonnaise

DIRECTIONS:

- ➤ Preheat the panini press.
- ➤ Spread butter on one side of each slice of bread.
- ➤ Take 4 slices of bread and spread with mayonnaise.
- ➤ Cover with beef, cheese, tomatoes and onion.
- ➤ Bake for 5 minutes or until golden brown.
- ➤ Cover with the remaining slices of bread.
- ➤ Make sure the buttered side up.
- ➤ Place 2 sandwiches on a hot Panini press.
- ➤ Close and press Panini

10. BLEU ROAST BEEF PANINI

Servings:1 **Cooking Time: 4 Minutes** **Prep.Time: 10 Minutes**

INGREDIENT

- ✓ 2 slices multigrain bread
- ✓ 1 tablespoon mayonnaise (chipotle)
- ✓ 1 -2 slice provolone cheese (picante)
- ✓ 1/4 cup blue cheese, crumbled
- ✓ 4 slices roast beef
- ✓ 1/8 cup red onion, diced
- ✓ Nonstick cooking spray

DIRECTIONS

- ➤ Fry the diced red onion until soft.
- ➤ Set a waffle iron on high until a little smoke appears.
- ➤ Wait for the waffle iron to heat up.
- ➤ Assemble the sandwiches
- ➤ Starting with the mayonnaise
- ➤ Then adding the next four ingredients.
- ➤ Be ready for the waffle iron to start smoking
- ➤ Lower the heat to medium
- ➤ Heat and spray with non-stick spray.
- ➤ Cook the sandwich in the waffle iron for 3-4 minutes.
- ➤ Enjoy your meal!

11. *GRILL COD* PANINI

Servings:4   Cook. Time:8 Minutes   Prep.Time: 10 Minute

INGREDIENTS:
- 4 cod fillets
- 1 tbsp olive oil
- 2 tbsp blackened seasoning
- 1/2 tsp kosher salt

DIRECTIONS:
- Preheat the Panini press.
- Brush the cod fillets with oil
- Season with blackened seasoning and kosher salt.
- Place the fish fillets on the hot Panini press
- Cook for 4 minutes on each side.
- Serve and enjoy

12. *GRILLED CHEESE PANINI*

Servings:2   Cook. Time:5 Minutes   Prep.Time: 5 Minute

INGREDIENTS

- 4 bread slices
- 4 oz. mozzarella
- 2 oz. feta cheese

- 2 tsp basil
- 2 tablespoons butter

DIRECTIONS

- Put the onions, honey, Dijon and vinegar in a saucepan;
- Cook stirring over medium heat until onions are tender
- Time about 8-10 minutes
- Afterwards season with black pepper.
- Butter both sides of bread.

- Top 4 slices of bread with the roast beef,
- Then 2 slices of cheese and 1/4 of the onion mixture.
- Top with the remaining slice of bread.
- Heat up an electric sandwich machine
- Place a sandwich in
- Close lid; heat until golden brown.

13. *PANINI WITH GRILLED PINEAPPLE SLICES*

Servings:4   Cook. Time:12 Minutes   Prep.Time: 10 Minute

INGREDIENTS

- 4 pineapple slices
- 1 tbsp olive oil

- Salt

DIRECTIONS

- Preheat the panini press.
- Brush the pineapple slices with oil and season with salt.

- Place the pineapple slices on the hot Panini press and
- Cook for 5-6 minutes on each side.

14. GRILLED BEEF AND ONION PANINI

Servings:4   **Cook. Time:12 Minutes**   **Prep.Time: 20 Minute**

INGREDIENTS

- ✓ 3 sweet onions, thinly sliced
- ✓ 2 tablespoons honey
- ✓ 1 tablespoon Dijon mustard
- ✓ 1 tablespoon apple cider vinegar
- ✓ black pepper

- ✓ softened butter
- ✓ 8 slices rye bread (or use pumpernickel bread)
- ✓ 3/4 lb thinly-sliced deli roast beef
- ✓ 8 slices American chees

DIRECTIONS

- ➢ Put the onions, honey, Dijon and vinegar in a saucepan;
- ➢ Cook stirring over medium heat until onions are tender
- ➢ Time about 8-10 minutes
- ➢ Then season with black pepper.
- ➢ Butter both sides of the bread.
- ➢ Top 4 slices of bread with the roast beef,

- ➢ Then 2 slices of cheese and 1/4 of the onion mixture.
- ➢ Top with the remaining slice of bread.
- ➢ Heat up an electric sandwich machine
- ➢ Place a sandwich in
- ➢ Close the lid; heat until golden brownPlace the pineapple slices on the hot sandwich press and
- ➢ Cook for 5-6 minutes on each side

15. GRILLED PANINI WHIT BACON CHEDDAR & TOMATO

Servings:4   **Cook. Time:12 Minutes**   **Prep.Time: 20 Minute**

INGREDIENTS

- ✓ 4 roma tomatoes, halved lengthwise
- ✓ pulp and seeds removed
- ✓ olive oil
- ✓ coarse sea salt
- ✓ fresh ground black pepper
- ✓ 8 basil leaves, thinly sliced

- ✓ 2 tablespoons unsalted butter, melted
- ✓ 8 slices sourdough bread
- ✓ 8 slices bacon, fully cooked*
- ✓ 4 ounces sharp cheddar cheese, thinly sliced

DIRECTIONS

- ➢ Preheat the panini grill to high heat.
- ➢ Make sure the grill is slightly tilted
- ➢ Make sure to attach the drip tray.
- ➢ Brush the cut side of the tomatoes with olive oil.
- ➢ Season with salt and pepper.
- ➢ Place the tomatoes, cut side down, on the Panini grill
- ➢ Lower the upper grill just above the tomatoes without touching them.
- ➢ Grill the tomatoes for 10-12 minutes.
- ➢ Wait until the outer skins are wrinkled and the tomatoes are soft.

- ➢ Check the tomatoes often,
- ➢ because some may cook faster than others.
- ➢ Remove the tomatoes from the grill and sprinkle with basil.
- ➢ Brush melted butter on the outer sides of each slice of bread.
- ➢ For each sandwich, layer two slices of bacon, two grilled tomatoes, and one grilled tomato.
- ➢ Add 1/4 of the cheese between two slices of bread (buttered side out).
- ➢ Grill the sandwich for 5-7 minutes
- ➢ Wait until the cheese is melted and the bread is toasted

16. CREAM CHEESE APPLE PANINI

Servings:2   **Cook. Time:15 Minutes**   **Prep.Time: 10 Minute**

INGREDIENTS
- ✓ 1 egg
- ✓ 4 whole-wheat bread slices
- ✓ 4 tbsp cream cheese, softened
- ✓ 1/4 cup milk
- ✓ 1 egg whites
- ✓ 1 apple, thinly sliced

DIRECTIONS
- ➢ Add the apple slices to the microwave dish and microwave for 4-5 minutes.
- ➢ In a large bowl, whisk the eggs with the milk.
- ➢ Preheat the Panini press.
- ➢ Spread 1 tablespoon of cream cheese on each slice of bread.
- ➢ Take 2 slices of bread and stuff the sides of the cream cheese with the sliced apples to make a sandwich.
- ➢ Dip the egg in the sandwich and place it on a hot press.
- ➢ Close the panini press and bake for 4-5 minutes or until golden brown.
- ➢ Serve and enjoy

17. ARUGULA BACON CHEESE PANINI

Servings:1   **Cook. Time:5 Minutes**   **Prep.Time: 10 Minute**

INGREDIENTS
- ✓ 2 bread slices
- ✓ 1/4 cup arugula
- ✓ 1 fried egg
- ✓ 2 bacon slices, cooked
- ✓ 3 tbsp cheddar cheese, grated

DIRECTIONS
- ➢ Take a slice of bread and sprinkle it with cheese.
- ➢ Then top with the bacon slices, egg and rocket.
- ➢ Cover with the remaining slice of bread.
- ➢ Preheat the Panini press.
- ➢ Spray the sandwiches with cooking spray.
- ➢ Place them on a hot Panini press.
- ➢ Close panini press
- ➢ Bake for 4-5 minutes or until golden brown.
- ➢ Serve and enjoy

18. BALSAMIC RED ONION GRUYERE PANINI/GRILLED CHEESE

Servings:4　　　　**Cook. Time:15 Minutes**　　　　**Prep.Time: 5 Minute**

INGREDIENTS

- ✓ 1 red onion, thinly sliced
- ✓ 1 tablespoon balsamic vinegar (or to taste)
- ✓ 1/2 tablespoon olive oil
- ✓ 1 pinch salt
- ✓ 1 teaspoon sugar
- ✓ 8 slices sourdough bread
- ✓ 4 ounces gruyere cheese, shredded
- ✓ white truffle oil (optional)

DIRECTIONS

- ➢ Put the onions, balsamic vinegar, oil, salt and sugar in a saucepan,
- ➢ cover and cook over a medium-low heat until very soft.
- ➢ The onions should still be purple
- ➢ (if they are black there is probably too much vinegar).
- ➢ Remember that you can always add more but you can't remove it.
- ➢ Put the cheese and onion together on the bread.
- ➢ Drizzle with truffle oil and grill in a frying pan or Panini press.
- ➢ Dunk in tomato and basil soup

19. CAPRESE PANINI

Servings:4　　　　**Cook. Time:5 Minutes**　　　　**Prep.Time: 5 Minute**

INGREDIENTS

- ✓ 4 bread slices
- ✓ 1 tomato
- ✓ 4 slices mozzarella cheese
- ✓ ¼ cup basil leaves
- ✓ 1 tsp olive oil

DIRECTIONS

- ➢ Prepare the bread for the sandwiches
- ➢ Place all the ingredients on one slice of bread
- ➢ Cover with the other slice of bread
- ➢ Toast the sandwich until golden brown
- ➢ Serve when ready

20. GOAT CHEESE PANINI

Servings:4　　　　**Cook. Time:5 Minutes**　　　　**Prep.Time: 5 Minute**

INGREDIENTS

- ✓ 4 bread slices
- ✓ 2 oz. goat cheese
- ✓ ¼ cup baby spinach
- ✓ ½ cup red peppers
- ✓ 2 tablespoons butter

DIRECTIONS

- ➢ Prepare the bread for the sandwiches
- ➢ Place all the ingredients on one slice of bread
- ➢ Cover with the other slice of bread
- ➢ Toast the sandwich until golden brown
- ➢ Serve when ready

21. ITALIAN MOZZARELLA BREAKFAST PANINI

Servings:1　　　　**Cook. Time:5 Minutes**　　　　**Prep.Time: 10 Minute**

INGREDIENTS

- ✓ 1 flatbread
- ✓ 3 basil leaves
- ✓ 1 tomato, sliced
- ✓ 1 oz mozzarella cheese, sliced
- ✓ 2 eggs, scrambled

DIRECTIONS

- ➢ Preheat the Panini press.
- ➢ Fold the focaccia and stuff it with the scrambled egg.
- ➢ Add the egg, cheese, tomato slices and basil.
- ➢ Spray the sandwich with cooking spray.
- ➢ Place on a hot Panini press.
- ➢ Close the Panini press
- ➢ Bake for 4-5 minutes or until golden brown.

22. BASIC GRILLED CHEESE PANINI

Servings:2   **Cook. Time:5 Minutes**   **Prep.Time:15 Minute**

INGREDIENTS
- ✓ 2 tablespoons butter, softened
- ✓ 2 slices of your favorite bread
- ✓ 2 slices of your favorite cheese

DIRECTIONS
- ➤ Butter the bread slices on 1 side. Turn them over.
- ➤ Place the cheese slices on 1 slice of bread.
- ➤ Top with the other slice of bread, buttered side up.
- ➤ The buttered sides are facing outwards.
- ➤ Check that they become crispy and golden when they touch the hot pan.
- ➤ Heat a medium frying pan over medium heat.
- ➤ Pour a drop of water into the pan.
- ➤ If it sizzles and evaporates, the pan is hot enough.
- ➤ Place the buns, buttered side down, in the pan.
- ➤ Let it cook for 3 to 4 minutes
- ➤ (or until golden brown and crispy underneath).
- ➤ Using a spatula (or one in each hand, if the bread is large), turn the sandwich over.
- ➤ Let it cook another 3 to 4 minutes, or until golden brown and crispy on the second side.
- ➤ Choose a cheese that melts well.
- ➤ Here are some grilled cheeses: cheddar, jack and pepper jack, Colby
- ➤ Gruyère, Swiss, fontina, provolone. Brie also works well

23. FONTINA PANINI

Servings:2   **Cook. Time:5 Minutes**   **Prep.Time:5 Minute**

INGREDIENTS
- ✓ 4 bread slices
- ✓ 4 slices bacon
- ✓ 2 tablespoons mustard
- ✓ 8 oz. fontina cheese
- ✓ 1 red bell pepper

DIRECTIONS
- ➤ Prepare the bread for the sandwiches
- ➤ Place all the ingredients on one slice of bread
- ➤ Cover with the other slice of bread
- ➤ Toast the sandwich until golden brown
- ➤ Serve when ready

24. GORGONZOLA MAYO ROASTBEEF PANINI

Servings:4   **Cook. Time:10 Minutes**   **Prep.Time:10 Minute**

INGREDIENTS
- ✓ 8 bread slices
- ✓ 2 tbsp butter
- ✓ 8 fontina cheese slices
- ✓ 12 oz sweet roasted red peppers
- ✓ 4 oz baby spinach
- ✓ 1/4 cup gorgonzola cheese, crumbled
- ✓ 1 garlic clove, chopped
- ✓ 1/2 cup mayonnaise
- ✓ 3/4 lb deli roast beef, sliced

DIRECTIONS
- ➤ In a small bowl, mix the mayonnaise, gorgonzola and garlic.
- ➤ Preheat the Panini press.
- ➤ Spread butter on one side of each slice of bread.
- ➤ Take 4 slices of bread and spread with mayonnaise.
- ➤ Top with beef, spinach, roasted peppers and cheese.
- ➤ Cover with the remaining slices of bread.
- ➤ Make sure the buttered side up.
- ➤ Place 2 sandwiches on a hot press.
- ➤ Close the panini press and bake for 5 minutes.
- ➤ Wait or until golden brown.
- ➤ Serve and enjoy.

25. SPINACH ARTICHOKE PANINI

Servings:4   **Cook. Time:10 Minutes**   **Prep.Time:10 Minutes**

INGREDIENTS

- 8 bread slices
- 1 cup baby spinach
- 8 oz mozzarella cheese, shredded
- 12 oz grilled chicken strips
- 6.5 oz marinated artichoke hearts, chopped
- 1/4 cup cream cheese spread
- 2 tbsp butter

DIRECTIONS

- Preheat the panini press.
- Spread butter on one side of each slice of bread.
- Take 4 slices of bread and
- spread with cream cheese
- Top with artichoke hearts,
- Then chicken strips, spinach
- Add the mozzarella cheese.
- Cover with remaining bread slices.
- Make sure the buttered side is on top.
- Place 2 sandwiches on a hot press.
- Close the panini press.
- Bake for 4-5 minutes
- (or until golden brown).
- Serve and enjoy

26. SPINACH APPLE AND CHEESE PANINI

Servings:4   **Cook. Time:10 Minutes**   **Prep.Time:10 Minutes**

INGREDIENTS

- 1 teaspoon extra virgin olive oil
- 1 cup sliced yellow onion
- (or about 1/2 a large onion)
- 1 large ambrosia apple, thinly sliced and tossed with juice of 1 lime
- 1 cup spinach leaves, stems removed
- 4 ounces low-fat Swiss cheese, thinly sliced into 4 slices
- 8 slices whole wheat sourdough bread or 4 ciabatta rolls

DIRECTIONS

- Heat a medium saucepan
- Bring to a medium-high heat for 1 to 2 minutes.
- Add the oil and onions.
- Stir occasionally.
- After about 5 minutes, the onions will start to caramelise,
- You will need to stir constantly
- Time about 5 min.
- The onions should be evenly burnt brown.
- Remove from heat and set aside.
- Assemble the sandwiches
- Spread 2 tablespoons of onions on each of the 4 pieces of bread
- Top each slice with 4 spinach leaves,
- Then 1 slice of cheese

27. SPINACH TOMATO PANINI

Serving:1   **Cook. Time:5 Minutes**   **Prep.Time:10 Minutes**

INGREDIENTS

- ✓ 2 bread slices
- ✓ 1 cheese slice
- ✓ 1 cup frozen spinach, thawed & drained
- ✓ 1/2 tomato, sliced
- ✓ 1 tbsp tomato pesto
- ✓ 1 tbsp mayonnaise
- ✓ 2 tsp butter

DIRECTIONS

- ➤ Preheat the panini press.
- ➤ Spread butter on one side of each slice of bread.
- ➤ In a small bowl, mix together the mayonnaise and tomato pesto.
- ➤ Take 1 slice of bread and spread it with the mayonnaise mixture, then top with the tomato, spinach and cheese slice.
- ➤ Cover with the remaining slice of bread. Make sure the buttered side is on top.
- ➤ Place the sandwich on a hot Panini press.
- ➤ Close the Panini press and bake for 4-5 minutes or until golden brown.
- ➤ Serve and enjoy.

28. WAFFLE PANINI WITH CHEESE SPINACH AND SPICY MUSTARD

Servings:2   **Cook. Time:5 Minutes**   **Prep.Time:15 Minutes**

INGREDIENTS

- ✓ 1 roma (plum) tomato, thinly sliced
- ✓ salt and ground black pepper to taste
- ✓ 1 teaspoon spicy brown mustard
- ✓ 1 cup fresh spinach, or to taste
- ✓ 2 teaspoons chopped sweet onion
- ✓ 2 teaspoons butter, softened
- ✓ 4 thickly-sliced pieces multigrain bread
- ✓ 4 slices part-skim mozzarella cheese

DIRECTIONS

- ➤ Preheat a waffle iron
- ➤ Place the tomato slices on a work surface,
- ➤ Pour off any excess juice. Season the tomato
- ➤ Season the slices with salt and pepper.
- ➤ Spread 1/2 teaspoon of butter on 1 side of each slice of bread.
- ➤ Place 1 slice of bread, butter side down, in hot waffle iron.
- ➤ Spread 1/2 teaspoon of mustard on the slice of bread in the waffle iron;
- ➤ Add 1/4 cup spinach, 2 slices mozzarella cheese
- ➤ Add 1 teaspoon of onion, half of the tomato slices,
- ➤ Top with 1/4 cup spinach,
- ➤ Arrange 1 slice of bread with butter
- ➤ The butter should be facing upwards on top of the spinach layer
- ➤ Close the waffle iron
- ➤ Toast the sandwiches until lightly browned,
- ➤ Time about 2 minutes.
- ➤ Repeat with remaining ingredients

29. POTATO SPINACH PANINI

Servings:2 **Cook. Time:5 Minutes** **Prep.Time:10 Minutes**

INGREDIENTS
- ✓ 4 bread slices
- ✓ 1/2 cup spinach, cooked
- ✓ 1/2 cup mashed potatoes
- ✓ 2 tbsp mayonnaise
- ✓ 1 tbsp butter

DIRECTIONS
- ➢ Preheat the panini press.
- ➢ Spread butter on one side of each slice of bread.
- ➢ Take 2 slices of bread and spread with mayonnaise
- ➢ Then cover with mashed potatoes and spinach.
- ➢ Cover with the other slices of bread. Make sure that the buttered side is on top.
- ➢ Place the sandwiches on a hot Panini press.
- ➢ Close the Panini press and bake for 4-5 minutes or until golden brown.
- ➢ Serve and enjoy

30. SAUSAGE AND SPINACH PANINI

Servings:2 **Cook. Time:5 Minutes** **Prep.Time:10 Minutes**

INGREDIENTS
- ✓ Vegetable cooking spray
- ✓ 1 (4-ounce) Italian-flavored turkey sausage link, cut in half crosswise
- ✓ 4 cups torn spinach
- ✓ Dash of salt
- ✓ 2 (1 1/2-ounce) French bread rolls
- ✓ 1 garlic clove, halved
- ✓ 1 teaspoon olive oil
- ✓ 1/8 teaspoon ground red pepper

DIRECTIONS
- ➢ Coat a large non-stick frying pan with cooking spray,
- ➢ Place over a medium heat until hot.
- ➢ Add the sausage, c
- ➢ Cook 10 minutes, turning occasionally.
- ➢ Remove sausage from pan;
- ➢ Cut each piece in half lengthwise,
- ➢ Cut on the other side but not through
- ➢ Open the halves, laying the sausage flat.
- ➢ Return the sausage to the frying pan,
- ➢ placing cut sides down;
- ➢ Cook 2 minutes or until sausage is done.
- ➢ Remove sausage from skillet;
- ➢ Set aside, and keep warm.
- ➢ Add spinach to skillet;
- ➢ Cover and cook 2 minutes or until wilted.
- ➢ Remove spinach from pan;
- ➢ Set aside and keep warm.
- ➢ Cut each roll of French bread in half horizontally.
- ➢ Rub the cut sides of the bread with the garlic halves,
- ➢ Brush with olive oil.
- ➢ Coat the pan with cooking spray,
- ➢ Place pan over medium-high heat until hot.
- ➢ Place the bread, cut sides down, in the pan,
- ➢ Cook for 1 minute or until toasted.
- ➢ Divide spinach between bottom halves of bread,
- ➢ Sprinkle with pepper and salt.
- ➢ Top each sandwich with the sausage,
- ➢ Cover with the top half of the bread

31. SPINACH PEAR FETA PANINI

Servings:2　　　　**Cook. Time:5 Minutes**　　　　**Prep.Time:10 Minutes**

INGREDIENTS

- ✓ 4 bread slices
- ✓ 1 tbsp vinegar
- ✓ 1 tbsp walnuts, toasted
- ✓ 1 tbsp fresh sage, chopped
- ✓ 1/2 cup baby spinach
- ✓ 2 oz feta cheese, crumbled
- ✓ 1 ripe pear, sliced thinly
- ✓ 2 tbsp cream cheese, softened
- ✓ 1 tbsp butter

DIRECTIONS

- ➢ Preheat the panini press.
- ➢ Spread butter on one side of each slice of bread.
- ➢ Take 2 slices of bread and
- ➢ Spread with cream cheese and then
- ➢ Top with pear, spinach, feta cheese, sage and walnuts. Sprinkle with vinegar.
- ➢ Cover with the other slices of bread.
- ➢ Make sure the buttered side up.
- ➢ Place the sandwiches in a hot panini press.
- ➢ Close the Panini
- ➢ Press and bake for 4-5 minutes
- ➢ (or until golden brown).
- ➢ Serve and enjoy.

32. TASTY AVOCADO SPINACH PANINI

Serving:1　　　　**Cook. Time:5 Minutes**　　　　**Prep.Time:10 Minutes**

INGREDIENTS

- ✓ 2 bread slices
- ✓ 6 spinach leaves
- ✓ 1/2 avocado, chopped
- ✓ 2 pepper jack cheese slices
- ✓ 2 tsp butter

DIRECTIONS

- ➢ Preheat the bread press.
- ➢ Spread butter on one side of each slice of bread.
- ➢ Take 1 slice of bread
- ➢ Cover with avocado, spinach and cheese.
- ➢ Cover with the remaining slice of bread.
- ➢ Make sure the buttered side up.
- ➢ Place the sandwich on a hot press.
- ➢ Close the sandwich press.
- ➢ Bake for 4-5 minutes
- ➢ (or until golden brown).
- ➢ Serve and enjoy.

33. BAKED TOFU PANINI WITH ROASTED PEPPERS AND SPINACH

Servings:4 **Cook. Time:1 H and 30 Min** **Prep.Time:15 Minutes**

INGREDIENTS

- ✓ Baked Marinated Tofu
- ✓ 2 tablespoons maple syrup
- ✓ 3 tablespoons reduced sodium soy sauce
- ✓ 1 teaspoon chili powder
- ✓ 1 teaspoon onion powder
- ✓ 1 teaspoon garlic powder
- ✓ 3 dashes liquid smoke (optional)
- ✓ salt and pepper
- ✓ 1/3 cup water
- ✓ 1 (14 ounce) package extra firm tofu

- ✓ (Sliced into 12-13 even slices)
- ✓ Caramelized Onions
- ✓ 5 large onions (yellow, red or white)
- ✓ 5 teaspoons olive oil
- ✓ 1 tablespoon balsamic vinegar
- ✓ 1 teaspoon sugar
- ✓ salt and pepper
- ✓ Sandwich
- ✓ 2 slices ciabatta
- ✓ 1 cup fresh spinach leaves
- ✓ 1 tablespoon hummus (Greek olive)

DIRECTIONS

- ➢ Caramelized onions
- ➢ Heat the oil in a large, heavy-bottomed frying pan.
- ➢ Keep the heat on medium-high until the oil is shimmering.
- ➢ Add the onion slices
- ➢ Stir to coat the onions with the oil.
- ➢ Spread the onions evenly over the pan.
- ➢ Leave to cook, stirring occasionally.
- ➢ After 10 minutes, sprinkle the onions over the top.
- ➢ If the onions dry out, you can add a touch of vegan butter.
- ➢ Reduce the heat to medium low.
- ➢ Leave to cook for 30 to 60 minutes or more.
- ➢ Stirring every few minutes
- ➢ When onions are almost cooked, deglaze with vinegar.

- ➢ Roast sweet red peppers
- ➢ Cut the peppers so that they are long and slightly thin and seedless.
- ➢ Spray a baking sheet with cooking spray.
- ➢ Place on the sheet, spraying again with cooking spray
- ➢ Add lightly with sea salt and pepper
- ➢ Place in oven at 395 degrees for about 30 minutes
- ➢ (or so, flipping ½ way through)
- ➢ Bake until soft-tender.
- ➢ Assemble and press!
- ➢ Wrap the sandwich in foil
- ➢ Place in the oven under a cast iron pan
- ➢ (or a clean brick wrapped in foil).
- ➢ Ideal time 20 min

34. PANINI WITH SPINACH SAUTÉED AND CHICKPEAS SPREAD

Servings:4   **Cook. Time:1 H and 30 Min**   **Prep.Time:15 Minutes**

INGREDIENTS

- ✓ 3/4 cup chickpeas (garbanzo beans)
- ✓ 2 tablespoons lemon juice
- ✓ 1 tablespoon water
- ✓ 2 teaspoons capers
- ✓ 2 teaspoons olive oil
- ✓ 2 garlic cloves, minced
- ✓ 4 cups torn spinach
- ✓ 1/8 teaspoon pepper
- ✓ 2 (2 1/2-ounce) submarine rolls

DIRECTIONS

- ➢ Place the first 4 ingredients in a food processor,
- ➢ Process until smooth, scraping down the sides of the processor bowl
- ➢ Heat oil in a large non-stick frying pan over medium heat.
- ➢ Add garlic; sauté 1 minute.
- ➢ Add spinach; sauté 1 minute.
- ➢ Remove pan from heat and stir in pepper.
- ➢ Cut each roll in half horizontally.
- ➢ Spread the chickpea mixture over the bottom half of the bread.
- ➢ Cover with spinach
- ➢ Cover with the top half of the bread.

35. SPINACH PESTO CHICKEN PANINI

Servings:4   **Cook. Time10 Minutes**   **Prep.Time:10 Minutes**

INGREDIENTS

- ✓ 8 bread slices
- ✓ 8 Swiss cheese slices
- ✓ 1 cup baby spinach
- ✓ 1 1/2 cups chicken breast, cooked & shredded
- ✓ 2 tbsp pesto
- ✓ 1/2 cup mayonnaise
- ✓ 2 tbsp butter
- ✓ Pepper
- ✓ Salt

DIRECTIONS

- ➢ Preheat the panini press.
- ➢ Spread butter on one side of each slice of bread.
- ➢ In a bowl, mix chicken, mayo, pesto, pepper, salt.
- ➢ Take 4 slices of bread
- ➢ Cover with chicken mixture, spinach and cheese.
- ➢ Cover with remaining bread slices.
- ➢ Make sure the buttered side up.
- ➢ Place 2 sandwiches on a hot press.
- ➢ Close the panini press.
- ➢ Bake for 5 minutes
- ➢ (or until golden brown).

36. SIMPLE SPINACH PANINI

Servings:2   **Cook. Time:5 Minutes**   **Prep.Time:5 Minutes**

INGREDIENTS

- ✓ 1 Cup of Spinach
- ✓ 2 fried eggs
- ✓ ¼ cup red peppers
- ✓ ¼ cup arugula
- ✓ 3-4 slices cheese
- ✓ 4 bread slices

DIRECTIONS

- ➢ Prepare the bread for the sandwiches
- ➢ Place all the ingredients on one slice of bread
- ➢ Cover with the other slice of bread
- ➢ Toast the sandwich until golden brown.

37. EASY PORK PANINI

Servings:4   **Cook. Time:10 Minutes**   **Prep.Time:15 Minutes**

INGREDIENTS
- ✓ 8 bread slices
- ✓ 2 tbsp butter
- ✓ 4 oz provolone cheese slices
- ✓ 1/2 cup pesto
- ✓ 3 pork chops, cooked & sliced

DIRECTIONS
- ➤ Preheat the panini press.
- ➤ Spread butter on one side of each slice of bread.
- ➤ Take 4 slices of bread and spread
- ➤ spread with pesto
- ➤ top with the pork and cheese.
- ➤ Cover with the remaining bread slices.
- ➤ Make sure the buttered side is on top.
- ➤ Place 2 sandwiches on a hot press.
- ➤ Close the sandwich press.
- ➤ Bake for 5 minutes
- ➤ (or until golden brown).
- ➤ Serve and enjoy

38. CUBANPORK PANINI

Serving:1   **Cook. Time:5 Minutes**   **Prep.Time:10 Minutes**

INGREDIENTS
- ✓ 2 bread slices
- ✓ 1 tbsp butter
- ✓ 1 roasted pork slice
- ✓ 2 ham slices
- ✓ 1 fontina cheese slice
- ✓ 1 Swiss cheese slice
- ✓ 2 tbsp sweet banana peppers, sliced
- ✓ 2 tbsp jalapeno peppers, sliced
- ✓ 2 tbsp honey mustard

DIRECTIONS
- ➤ Preheat the bread press.
- ➤ Spread butter on one side of each slice of bread.
- ➤ Take 1 slice of bread
- ➤ Spread with honey mustard
- ➤ Top with pork slice, jalapeno peppers
- ➤ Add the banana sweet peppers, the ham, the cheese.
- ➤ Cover with the remaining slice of bread.
- ➤ Make sure the butter side is on top.
- ➤ Place the sandwiches on a hot press.
- ➤ Close the sandwich press.
- ➤ Bake for 5 minutes
- ➤ (or until golden brown).

39. PORK CHEDDAR APPLE PANINI

Serving:1   Cook. Time:5 Minutes   Prep.Time:10 Minutes

INGREDIENTS

- ✓ 8 pork chops, boneless, cooked & sliced
- ✓ 4 oz cheddar cheese, sliced
- ✓ 1 apple, core & slice
- ✓ 3 tbsp butter

- ✓ 8 bread slices
- ✓ 2 tbsp Dijon mustard
- ✓ 4 tbsp apricot preserves

DIRECTIONS

- ➢ Preheat the panini press.
- ➢ Spread butter on one side of each slice of bread.
- ➢ Take 4 slices of bread
- ➢ Spread with Dijon mustard
- ➢ Add apricot preserves
- ➢ Cover with pork, apple and cheese.

- ➢ Cover with remaining bread slices.
- ➢ Make sure the buttered side is on top.
- ➢ Place 2 sandwiches on a hot press.
- ➢ Close the sandwich press
- ➢ And bake for 5 minutes
- ➢ (Or until golden brown).

40. BBQ PORK PANINI SANDWICH

Servings:4   Cook. Time: 1h 35 Mins   Prep.Time:1h 20 Mins

INGREDIENTS

- ✓ 3⁄4 cup white sugar
- ✓ 1 1⁄2 cups paprika
- ✓ 3 3⁄4 tablespoons onion powder
- ✓ 3 lbs roast pork loin
- ✓ 4 tablespoons butter, room temperature
- ✓ 1 garlic clove, minced

- ✓ 4 french style sandwich buns, sliced horizontally
- ✓ dill pickle slices
- ✓ 1/4 lb sliced cheddar and colby cheese
- ✓ 1⁄2 cup barbecue sauce

DIRECTIONS

- ➢ Mix the rub ingredients in a bowl.
- ➢ Place the pork in an ovenproof dish.
- ➢ Rub the seasoning into the pork until it is covered.
- ➢ Cover with plastic wrap.
- ➢ Refrigerate to marinate for 1 hour.
- ➢ Preheat the oven to 325 degrees F.
- ➢ Place the pork roast in the oven.
- ➢ Bake for 1 1/2 hours.
- ➢ When cooked, tent roast with foil so juices settle.
- ➢ Slice thinly.

- ➢ Preheat panini press.
- ➢ In a small bowl mix butter and garlic.
- ➢ Butter the panini bread.
- ➢ Divide pork, evenly
- ➢ Place the pickles, cheese and barbecue sauce between the bread.
- ➢ Place the sandwiches in the press
- ➢ Close the lid.
- ➢ Grill the bread toasted
- ➢ Wait for the cheese to melt.
- ➢ Slice diagonally and serve hot

41. PULLED PORK PANINI

Servings:6   Cook. Time: 15 Minutes   Prep.Time:10 Minutes

INGREDIENTS
- ✓ 12 bread slices
- ✓ 4 tbsp butter
- ✓ 8 oz Colby Jack cheese, shredded
- ✓ 1 lb cooked pork, shredded
- ✓ 1/2 cup hot sauce

DIRECTIONS
- ➤ Preriscaldare la pressa per panini.
- ➤ Spalmare il burro su un lato di ogni fetta di pane.
- ➤ Prendere 6 fette di pane e
- ➤ Spalmare con la salsa piccante
- ➤ Coprire con carne di maiale e formaggio.
- ➤ Coprire con le fette di pane rimanenti.
- ➤ Assicurarsi che il lato imburrato sia in cima.
- ➤ Mettere 2 panini su una pressa caldaChiudere la pressa per panini
- ➤ Cuocere per 5 minuti
- ➤ (o fino a doratura).

42. GREEK PORK PANINI WITH OLIVES TAPENADE

Servings:2   Cook. Time: 5 Minutes   Prep.Time:10 Minutes

INGREDIENTS
- ✓ 4 bread slices
- ✓ 2 oz cheddar cheese, sliced
- ✓ 2 tbsp olive tapenade
- ✓ 6 oz porchetta
- ✓ 1 tbsp butter

DIRECTIONS
- ➤ Preheat the panini press.
- ➤ Spread butter on one side of each slice of bread.
- ➤ Take 2 slices of bread and cover them with
- ➤ cover with the olive tapenade, porchetta and cheese.
- ➤ Cover with the other slices of bread.
- ➤ Make sure the buttered side is on top.
- ➤ Place the sandwiches on a hot press.
- ➤ Close the sandwich press.
- ➤ Bake for 5 minutes
- ➤ (or until golden brown)

43. GRILL MARINADE PORK CHOPS PANINI

Servings:2   Cook. Time: 14 Minutes   Prep.Time:10 Minutes

INGREDIENTS
- ✓ 2 pork chops
- ✓ For marinade:
- ✓ 1/3 cup olive oil
- ✓ 1/2 tsp oregano
- ✓ 1 tsp onion powder
- ✓ 1 tbsp brown sugar
- ✓ 1/4 cup soy sauce
- ✓ 1/4 cup fresh lemon juice
- ✓ Pepper
- ✓ Salt

DIRECTIONS
- ➤ Add all the marinade ingredients to the ziplock bag.
- ➤ Mix thoroughly and well.
- ➤ Add the pork chops to the ziplock bag,
- ➤ Seal the bag by shaking well
- ➤ Refrigerate overnight.
- ➤ Preheat the panini press.
- ➤ Place the pork chops on the hot press and cook for 7 minutes on each side.
- ➤ Cook for 7 minutes on each side
- ➤ Serve and enjoy

44. EASY BANANA PEANUT BUTTER PANINI

Serving:1   Cook. Time: 5 Minutes   Prep.Time:10 Minutes

INGREDIENTS
- ✓ 2 bread slices
- ✓ 1/4 tsp ground cinnamon
- ✓ 1 tbsp honey
- ✓ 1/2 banana, cut into slices
- ✓ 4 tbsp peanut butter

DIRECTIONS
- ➤ Take a slice of bread
- ➤ spread with butter
- ➤ Then place the banana slices on top.
- ➤ Drizzle with honey. Sprinkle with cinnamon.
- ➤ Cover with the remaining bread.
- ➤ Preheat the Panini press.
- ➤ Spray the sandwich with cooking spray.
- ➤ Place on hot Panini press.
- ➤ Close panini press
- ➤ Bake for 4-5 minutes
- ➤ (or until golden brown)
- ➤ Serve and enjoy

45. AVOCADO CHICKPEAS PANINI

Servings:4   Cook. Time: 10 Minutes   Prep.Time:10 Minutes

INGREDIENTS
- ✓ 8 bread slices
- ✓ 1 cup baby spinach
- ✓ 1 tomato, sliced
- ✓ 1 tbsp fresh lemon juice
- ✓ 2 tbsp onion, diced
- ✓ 1/4 cup basil pesto
- ✓ 1 avocado
- ✓ 15 oz can chickpeas, drained & rinsed
- ✓ 2 tbsp butter
- ✓ Salt

DIRECTIONS
- ➤ In a bowl, mash the avocado and chickpeas.
- ➤ Use a potato masher.
- ➤ Add the pesto, onion, lemon juice, salt and
- ➤ salt and mix well.
- ➤ Preheat the Panini press.
- ➤ Spread butter on one side of each slice of bread.
- ➤ Take 4 slices of bread
- ➤ Spread with the avocado mixture.
- ➤ Add the tomatoes and spinach.
- ➤ Cover with the remaining bread slices.
- ➤ Make sure the buttered side is on top.
- ➤ Place 2 sandwiches on a hot Panini press.
- ➤ Close the Panini press and
- ➤ Bake for 4-5 minutes
- ➤ (or until golden brown).
- ➤ Serve and enjoy

46. WHITE CHEDDAR AND APRICOT PANINI

Servings:4   Cook. Time: 10 Minutes   Prep.Time:10 Minutes

INGREDIENTS
- ✓ 1 tablespoon apricot jam
- ✓ 2 slices bread
- ✓ 2 ounces thinly sliced white Cheddar
- ✓ 1/2 tablespoon butter

DIRECTIONS
- ➤ Spread the jam on 1 side of the sliced bread.
- ➤ Add Cheddar.
- ➤ Add a second slice of bread.
- ➤ Spread 1/4 tablespoon of butter on each side of the sandwich.
- ➤ Heat in a frying pan over medium heat.
- ➤ Wait for the cheese to melt
- ➤ Cook 2 minutes per side

47. STRAWBERRY CHEESE BRUSCHETTA

Servings:8　　　　　**Cook. Time: 10 Minutes**　　　　　**Prep.Time:10 Minutes**

INGREDIENTS
- ✓ 8 oz baguette bread, cut into 1-inch slices
- ✓ 2 tbsp olive oil
- ✓ For topping:
- ✓ 2 tbsp balsamic glaze
- ✓ 1 tbsp basil, chopped
- ✓ 1/2 cup goat cheese, crumbled
- ✓ 1/2 cup strawberries, sliced
- ✓ Pepper and Salt

DIRECTIONS
- ➤ Brush the slices of bread with oil and
- ➤ Place on a hot press. In batches.
- ➤ Close the panini press
- ➤ Bake for 8-10 minutes
- ➤ (or until golden brown).
- ➤ In a bowl, add all the topping ingredients and mix well.
- ➤ Spread the seasoning mixture over the toasted bread slices.
- ➤ Serve.

48. STRAWBERRY TURKEY BRIE PANINI

Servings:4　　　　　**Cook. Time: 10 Minutes**　　　　　**Prep.Time:10 Minutes**

INGREDIENTS
- ✓ 1 (8-oz.) Brie round
- ✓ 8 Italian bread slices
- ✓ 8 ounces thinly sliced smoked turkey
- ✓ 8 fresh basil leaves
- ✓ 1/2 cup sliced fresh strawberries
- ✓ 2 tablespoons red pepper jelly
- ✓ 2 tablespoons butter, melted
- ✓ Garnish: strawberry halves

DIRECTIONS
- ➤ Cut and discard the rind from the Brie.
- ➤ Cut the Brie into half-inch-thick slices.
- ➤ Layer 4 slices of bread evenly with the turkey,
- ➤ Place the basil leaves, strawberries and Brie on top.
- ➤ Spread 1 1/2 tablespoons pepper jelly on 1 side of each of the remaining 4 slices of bread;
- ➤ Place the bread slices, jelly sides down, on top of the Brie.
- ➤ Brush the sandwiches with melted butter.
- ➤ Bake the sandwiches in batches, in a preheated press
- ➤ Waiit for 2 to 3 minutes
- ➤ (or until golden brown).
- ➤ Garnish, if desired

Note: For testing purposes only, we used Braswell's Red Pepper Jelly. To prepare sandwiches without a Panini press, cook in a preheated grill pan over medium-high heat 2 to 3 minutes on each side or until golden

49. ORANGE CHICKEN PANINI

Serving:1   Cook. Time: 10 Minutes   Prep.Time:10 Minutes

INGREDIENTS

- ✓ 2 slices whole wheat bread or 2 slices rye bread
- ✓ (Or 2 slices white bread or 2 slices sourdough bread)
- ✓ 1 teaspoon mayonnaise
- ✓ 2 slices cooked turkey
- ✓ (Or 2 slices cooked chicken)
- ✓ 2 slices mozzarella cheese
- ✓ 1 orange, 3 segments used
- ✓ cilantro
- ✓ salt

DIRECTIONS

- ➤ Coat the inside of the bread slices with mayonnaise,
- ➤ Layer the chicken, cheese and orange segments on the bread.
- ➤ Sprinkle with coriander and salt.
- ➤ Prepare the sandwich machine
- ➤ follow the machine's instructions

50. EASY LEMON PEPPER CHICKEN PANINI

Servings:6   Cook. Time: 20 Minutes   Prep.Time:10 Minutes

INGREDIENTS

- ✓ 6 chicken breast, boneless
- ✓ 2 tsp garlic, minced
- ✓ 1/2 cup olive oil
- ✓ 2 lemon juice
- ✓ 1/2 onion, diced
- ✓ 1 tsp pepper
- ✓ 1 tsp salt

DIRECTIONS

- ➤ Add all the ingredients except the chicken to the ziplock bag.
- ➤ Mix well.
- ➤ Add the chicken to the bag,
- ➤ seal the bag
- ➤ Shake well and refrigerate overnight.
- ➤ Preheat the Panini press.
- ➤ Place chicken on hot Panini press.
- ➤ Cook for 20 minutes on each side.
- ➤ Turn the chicken breast over after every 5 minutes.
- ➤ Serve and enjoy.

51. LEMON PEPPER SALMON PANINI

Servings:4   Cook. Time: 8 Minutes   Prep.Time:10 Minutes

INGREDIENTS

- ✓ 1 1/2 lbs salmon fillets
- ✓ 1/4 cup olive oil
- ✓ 1 lemon juice
- ✓ 1 tsp dried oregano
- ✓ 2 garlic cloves, minced
- ✓ 1/2 tsp pepper
- ✓ 1 tsp sea salt

DIRECTIONS

- ➤ In a large bowl, mix oregano, garlic, olive oil, lemon juice and salt.
- ➤ Add pepper and salt.
- ➤ Then the salmon fillets and coat well.
- ➤ Cover and refrigerate for 15 minutes.
- ➤ Preheat the Panini press.
- ➤ Place the marinated salmon fillets on the hot Panini press.
- ➤ Cook for 4 minutes on each side.
- ➤ Serve and enjoy.

52. BECON AND CHEESE PANINI

Servings: 2   **Prep.Time: 5 Minutes**   **Cook Time 5 Minutes**

INGREDIENTS

- ✓ ¼ tsp salt
- ✓ 1 cup cheese
- ✓ 1 package bacon

- ✓ 4 slices bread
- ✓ 1 fried egg

DIRECTIONS

- ➤ Prepare the bread for the sandwiches
- ➤ Place all the ingredients on one slice of bread
- ➤ Cover with the other slice of bread

- ➤ Toast the sandwich until golden brown
- ➤ Serve when ready

53. SCRAMBLE EGG BREAKFAST PANINI

Servings: 4   **Prep.Time 10 Minutes**   **Cook time 15 Minutes**

INGREDIENTS:

- ✓ 4 eggs
- ✓ 1 tbsp olive oil
- ✓ 1/4 cup salsa

- ✓ 4 cheddar cheese slices
- ✓ 8 French bread slices
- ✓ 1 mango, peel & sliced thinly

DIRECTIONS:

- ➤ Spray the pan with cooking spray and heat over medium heat.
- ➤ In a bowl, beat the eggs. Pour the eggs into the hot pan and cook until set and stirred to scramble.
- ➤ Preheat panini press.
- ➤ Add 1/4 of the scrambled eggs to 4 slices of bread, then add mango slices, salsa and more bread slices.

- ➤ Brush outer sides of bread with oil and place on hot Panini press.
- ➤ Close the Panini press and bake until golden brown.
- ➤ Serve and enjoy.

54. BREAKFAST APPLE PANINI

Servings: 2   **Prep.Time: 10 Minutes**   **Cook Time 5 Minutes**

INGREDIENTS:

- ✓ 4 bread slices
- ✓ 1 cup gruyere cheese, shredded
- ✓ 1 cup cheddar cheese, shredded
- ✓ 2 tsp thyme leaves

- ✓ 2 apples, cored and sliced thinly
- ✓ 1 tbsp honey
- ✓ 2 tbsp Dijon mustard
- ✓ 2 tbsp butter, melted

DIRECTIONS:

- ➤ Preheat the panini press.
- ➤ Brush butter on one side of each slice of bread.
- ➤ In a small bowl, whisk together the honey and mustard.
- ➤ Take 2 slices of bread and spread them with the honey mixture.

- ➤ Add the apple slices, thyme and cheese.
- ➤ Cover with the remaining bread.
- ➤ Place the sandwiches on a hot Panini press.
- ➤ Close the Panini by pressing them
- ➤ Bake for 5 minutes or until golden brown.

55. CHEESE MORNING PANINI

Servings :2   **Prep Time: 5 Minutes**   **Cook Time: 5 Minutes**

INGREDIENTS

- ✓ 2 eggs
- ✓ ¼ tsp salt
- ✓ 2 tablespoons chives
- ✓ 2 bagels
- ✓ 3-4 slices tomato
- ✓ 3-4 slices onion
- ✓ 2 slices ham

DIRECTIONS

- ➢ Prepare the bread for the sandwiches
- ➢ Place all the ingredients on one slice of bread
- ➢ Cover with the other slice of bread
- ➢ Toast the sandwich until golden brown
- ➢ Serve when ready

56. BUTTER PEANUT PUMPKIN PANINI

Servings :2   **Prep Time: 5 Minutes**   **Cook Time: 5 Minutes**

INGREDIENTS:

- ✓ 4 bread slices
- ✓ 1 banana, cut into slices
- ✓ 1 tsp ground cinnamon
- ✓ 1/2 tsp pumpkin pie spice
- ✓ 2 tbsp maple syrup
- ✓ 1/2 cup peanut butter
- ✓ 1/2 cup can pumpkin puree

DIRECTIONS:

- ➢ In a small bowl, mix the pumpkin puree, pumpkin pie spice, maple syrup and peanut butter.
- ➢ Spread 1 tablespoon of pumpkin puree mixture on each slice of bread.
- ➢ Take 2 slices of bread and cover with banana slices. Cover each slice of bread with the second slice of bread to create sandwiches.
- ➢ Preheat the panini press.
- ➢ Place the sandwiches on a hot Panini press.
- ➢ Close the press and bake for 4-5 minutes or until golden brown.
- ➢ Serve and enjoy.

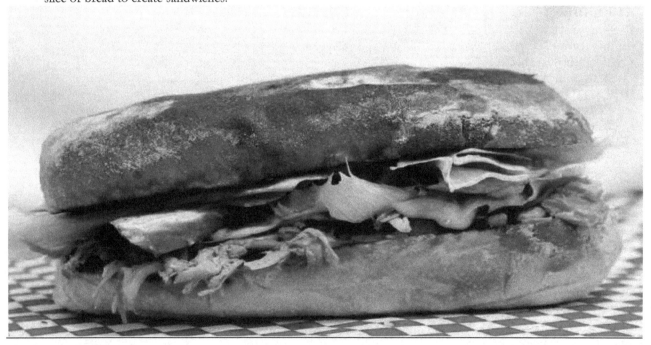

57. ORIGINAL TURKEY PANINI

Servings :2   **Prep Time: 5 Minutes**   **CookTime: 5 Minutes**

INGREDIENTS
- ✓ 2 slices bread
- ✓ 2 tablespoons mayonnaise
- ✓ 2 tablespoons guacamole
- ✓ 2 slices cheese
- ✓ 2 slices tomato

DIRECTIONS
- ➤ Prepare the bread for the sandwiches
- ➤ Place all the ingredients on one slice of bread
- ➤ Cover with the other slice of bread
- ➤ Toast the sandwich until golden brown
- ➤ Serve when ready

58. TURKEY SPINACH PANINI

Servings: 4   **Prep Time:10 Minutes**   **Cook Time: 10 Minutes**

INGREDIENTS:
- ✓ 1 lb ground turkey
- ✓ 1/2 cup feta cheese, crumbled
- ✓ 1 tbsp almond flour
- ✓ 1/4 tsp crushed red pepper
- ✓ 1 tsp parsley
- ✓ 1 tsp oregano
- ✓ 1 tsp garlic powder
- ✓ 1/3 cup sun-dried tomatoes
- ✓ 1/2 cup baby spinach, chopped
- ✓ 1/2 tsp pepper
- ✓ 1/2 tsp sea salt

DIRECTION:
- ➤ Preheat the panini press.
- ➤ Add all the ingredients to the mixing bowl and mix until well combined.
- ➤ Make 4 patties from the mixture and spray with cooking spray.
- ➤ Place the patties on the hot Panini press and cook for 5 minutes on each side.
- ➤ Serve and enjoy

59. SMOKED TURKEY PANINI

Servings: 2   **Prep Time:5 Minutes**   **Cook Time: 5 Minutes**

INGREDIENTS
- ✓ 4 bread slices
- ✓ 8 slices bacon
- ✓ 8 slices smoked turkey
- ✓ 4 oz. mayonnaise
- ✓ 2 cups baby spinach

DIRECTIONS
- ➤ Prepare the bread for the sandwiches
- ➤ Place all the ingredients on one slice of bread
- ➤ Cover with the other slice of bread
- ➤ Toast the sandwich until golden brown
- ➤ Serve when ready

60. EGGS AND WAFFEL PANINI

Servings: 4   **Prep Time:10 Minutes**   **Cook Time: 10 Minutes**

INGREDIENTS

- ✓ 2 waffles
- ✓ 2 eggs
- ✓ 2 tablespoon butters
- ✓ 2 slices cheddar cheese
- ✓ 2 breakfast sausage

DIRECTIONS

- ➢ Prepare the bread for the sandwiches
- ➢ Place all the ingredients on one slice of bread
- ➢ Cover with the other slice of bread
- ➢ Toast the sandwich until golden brown
- ➢ Serve when ready

61. EGGS TOMATO BACON PANINI

Servings: 2   **Prep Time:10 Minutes**   **Cook Time: 15 Minutes**

INGREDIENTS:

- ✓ 2 eggs
- ✓ 2 Swiss cheese slices
- ✓ 4 tomato slices
- ✓ 4 bacon slices, cooked
- ✓ 4 whole-wheat bread slices
- ✓ 2 tbsp butter
- ✓ 2 tbsp water
- ✓ Pepper
- ✓ Salt

DIRECTIONS:

- ➢ Spray the pan with cooking spray and heat over medium heat.
- ➢ In a bowl, beat the eggs with water, pepper and salt.
- ➢ Pour the eggs into the hot skillet and cook until set and stirred to scramble.
- ➢ Preheat the Panini press.
- ➢ Spread butter on one side of each slice of bread.
- ➢ Take 2 slices of bread and top with bacon, tomato slices, scrambled eggs and cheese, then cover with the remaining bread. Make sure the buttered side is on top.
- ➢ Place the sandwiches on a hot Panini press. Close the Panini press and bake for 4-5 minutes or until the cheese is melted.
- ➢ Serve and enjoy

62. EGGS AND BACON STRIPS PANINI

Servings: 2   **Prep.Time: 5 Minutes**   **Cook Time 5 Minutes**

INGREDIENTS

- ✓ 4 bacon strips
- ✓ 1 tsp butter
- ✓ 2 eggs
- ✓ 4 slices bread
- ✓ ¼ tsp salt
- ✓ 2 oz. cheese
- ✓ ¼ cup baby spinach

DIRECTIONS

- ➢ Prepare the bread for the sandwiches
- ➢ Place all the ingredients on one slice of bread
- ➢ Cover with the other slice of bread
- ➢ Toast the sandwich until golden brown.

63. EGGS AND SLICES BREAD PANINI

Servings: 2   **Prep Time:5 Minutes**   **Cook Time: 10 Minutes**

INGREDIENTS

- ✓ 4 bacon strips
- ✓ 2 tsp butter
- ✓ 4 eggs
- ✓ 4 slices bread
- ✓ ¼ tsp salt
- ✓ 4 oz. cheese
- ✓ ¼ cup baby spinach

DIRECTIONS

- ➤ Prepare the bread for the sandwiches
- ➤ Place all the ingredients on one slice of bread
- ➤ Cover with the other slice of bread
- ➤ Toast the sandwich until golden brown
- ➤ Serve when ready

64. EGGS AND POVOLONE CHEESE PANINI

Servings:: 2   **Prep Time:5 Minutes**   **Cook Time:10 Minutes**

INGREDIENTS

- ➤ 6 oz. provolone cheese
- ➤ 4 slices bread
- ➤ 8 slices prosciutto
- ➤ 4 eggs
- ➤ ¼ berry jam
- ➤ 2 tablespoons butter

DIRECTIONS

- ➤ Prepare the bread for the sandwiches
- ➤ Place all the ingredients on one slice of bread
- ➤ Cover with the other slice of bread
- ➤ Toast the sandwich until golden brown
- ➤ Serve when ready

65. VEGETARIAN AVOCADO PANINI

Servings: 4   **Prep.Time: 10 minutes**   **Cook.Time: 10 minutes**

INGREDIENTS:

- ✓ 8 whole-wheat bread slices
- ✓ 2 avocados
- ✓ 2 cups kale, chopped
- ✓ 1 cup cherry tomatoes
- ✓ 8 oz baby mushrooms, sliced
- ✓ 1 shallot, minced
- ✓ 1 1/2 tbsp butter
- ✓ Salt

DIRECTIONS:

- ➤ Melt the butter in a frying pan over medium-high heat.
- ➤ Add shallots and sauté until translucent.
- ➤ Add the mushrooms and sauté until lightly browned.
- ➤ Add the cabbage and tomatoes and cook until the cabbage is wilted. Remove the pan from the heat and season with salt.
- ➤ In a small bowl, mash the avocados with a fork.
- ➤ Take 4 slices of bread and spread them with the mashed avocado, then place the sautéed vegetables on top.
- ➤ Cover with the remaining slices of bread.
- ➤ Place 2 sandwiches on a hot Panini press.
- ➤ Close the Panini press and bake for 4-5 minutes or until golden brown.
- ➤ Serve and enjoy.

66. AVOCADO PESTO CHEESE PANINI

Servings:1   **Cooking Time: 5 Minutes**   **Prep.Time: 10 Minutes**

INGREDIENTS:

- ✓ 2 bread slices
- ✓ 4 tsp mayonnaise
- ✓ 1/2 avocado, sliced
- ✓ 3 mozzarella cheese slices
- ✓ 2 tbsp pesto

DIRECTIONS:

- ➤ Preheat the panini press.
- ➤ Spread the mayonnaise on one side of each slice of bread.
- ➤ Take 1 slice of bread and spread it with the pesto, then place the avocado and mozzarella slices on top.
- ➤ Cover with the remaining slice of bread. Make sure the mayonnaise side is on top.
- ➤ Place the sandwich on a hot Panini press.
- ➤ Close the Panini press and bake for 4-5 minutes or until golden brown.
- ➤ Serve and enjoy.

67. AVOCADO HAM PANINI

Servings:2   **Cooking Time: 5 Minutes**   **Prep.Time: 5 Minutes**

INGREDIENTS

- ✓ 4 bread slices
- ✓ 2 slices provolone cheese
- ✓ 3-4 slices avocado
- ✓ 8 slices of ham
- ✓ ¼ cup spinach
- ✓ 4-5 tomato slices

DIRECTIONS

- ✓ Prepare the bread for the sandwiches
- ✓ Place all the ingredients on one slice of bread
- ✓ Cover with the other slice of bread
- ✓ Toast the sandwich until golden brown
- ✓ Serve when ready

68. CHICKEN AND BACON PANINI WITH SPICY CHIP

Servings:2   **Cook. Time: 6 Minutes**   **Prep.Time: 20 Minutes**

INGREDIENTS

For the Spicy Chipotle Mayo
- ✓ 1 chipotle chile in adobo
- ✓ 1/2 cup mayonnaise

For the Panini
- ✓ 1 1/2 cups cooked chicken breasts
- ✓ 4 slices cooked bacon
- ✓ 1/2 cup shredded cheddar cheese (or more to taste)
- ✓ 1/2 tomatoes, sliced into 4 slices (can sub fresh avocado slices)

- ✓ 1 lime, juice of
- ✓ 1/2 teaspoon abodo seasoning

- ✓ 2 teaspoons olive oil
- ✓ salt
- ✓ 4 slices bread (something hearty like Italian

DIRECTIONS

- ➢ For the Spicy Chipotle Mayo:
- ➢ Add all ingredients into a food processor.
- ➢ Puree until smooth.
- ➢ Then salt and pepper to taste, if necessary.
- ➢ For the Panini: Turn on the oven to bake.
- ➢ Place the tomato slices on a lined baking tray.
- ➢ Drizzle with a little olive oil and sprinkle with salt.
- ➢ Place in the oven and roast the tomatoes until the top is slightly charred.
- ➢ Remove from the oven and set aside.
- ➢ (Note: this step can be skipped and replaced with avocado slices).
- ➢ Heat a Panini grill or frying pan over medium heat.

- ➢ Spread a little butter on one side of each piece of bread.
- ➢ Evenly distribute the chicken and cheese,
- ➢ place the bacon and tomatoes on two slices,
- ➢ Add the butter side down.
- ➢ On the other pieces of bread, spread a little chipotle mayonnaise on the unbuttered side.
- ➢ Place on top of the sandwich.
- ➢ Place the sandwich on the grill.
- ➢ Cook for about 2-3 minutes until the bread is golden brown.
- ➢ Gently flip the sandwich over.
- ➢ Bake for a further 2-3 minutes until the other side is golden brown.

69. CHICKEN AND AVOCADO PANINI

Servings:2   **Cooking Time: 10 Minutes**   **Prep.Time: 10 Minutes**

INGREDIENTS
- 1 avocado
- 1 teaspoon fresh lemon juice
- 1/4 cup red onion, diced
- 1/4 cup cilantro, chopped
- 1/3 cup grape tomatoes, quartered
- 2 teaspoons jalapenos, chopped
- Salt and pepper

- 2 pieces naan bread Add 4 pieces bacon, cooked crisp
- 1 cooked chicken breast half, sliced thin
- Usually used left over grilled or smoked
- 3 ounces monterey jack pepper cheese, sliced
- Usually half-light by Cabot
- 1 -2 teaspoon fat-free mayonnaise
- 1/4 cup fat-free cheddar cheese, grated

DIRECTIONS
- Heat the panini press to medium. .
- Peel and remove the core of the avocado.
- Coarsely mash the avocado in a bowl with a fork.
- Add the lemon juice and mix.
- Add the chopped onion, coriander and jalapeños,
- Add the tomatoes. Season with salt and pepper to taste.
- Spread a thin layer of mayonnaise on the bread slices.
- Assemble the sandwich by layering on the bread slices

- Add the jack cheese, the chicken
- then the bacon, the avocado mixture,
- then the grated cheddar.
- Cover with the remaining slice of bread.
- Grill until heated through.
- crispy on the outside.
- If using naan bread,
- slice into six triangles.
- If using other bread/tortilla,
- Cut according to the size of the sandwich

70. CHICKEN AND BRIE PANINI

Servings:2   **Cooking Time: 5 Minutes**   **Prep.Time: 5 Minutes**

INGREDIENTS
- 4 bread slices
- 1 chicken breast
- 1 onion

- 4 slices bacon
- 4 slices brie cheese
- 1/4 cup parsley

DIRECTIONS
- Prepare the bread for the sandwiches
- Place all the ingredients on one slice of bread
- Cover with the other slice of bread

- Toast the sandwich until golden brown
- Serve when ready

71. CHICKEN AND FONTINA PANINI

Servings:2   **Cooking Time: 4 Minutes**   **Prep.Time: 4 Minutes**

INGREDIENS
- 1 (8-oz.) loaf ciabatta bread, cut in half horizontally
- 3 tablespoons pesto sauce

- 2 plum tomatoes, sliced
- 1 cup shredded rotisserie chicken
- 2 slices fontina cheese

DIRECTIONS
- Preheat the Panini press.
- Spread the bottom half of the bread with pesto.
- Top with tomato slices, chicken and cheese.
- Top with bread.

- Place the sandwich in the Panini press;
- Bake 3 to 4 minutes or until cheese is melted and bread is toasted.
- Cut into quarters and serve hot

72. DELICIOUS PANERA FRONTEGA CHICKEN PANINI

Servings:2　　　　**Cook. Time: 10 Minutes**　　　　**Prep.Time: 10 Minutes**

INGREDIENTS:

- ✓ 4 bread slices
- ✓ 12 basil leaves, chopped
- ✓ 1/2 small onion, sliced
- ✓ 1 tomato, sliced
- ✓ 8 oz mozzarella ball, sliced
- ✓ 2 chicken breasts, cooked & shredded
- ✓ 1 chipotle pepper in adobo sauce
- ✓ 1/4 cup mayonnaise
- ✓ 1 tbsp butter

DIRECTIONS:

- ➢ Add the chipotle pepper and mayonnaise to a blender.
- ➢ Then blend until smooth.
- ➢ Preheat the Panini press.
- ➢ Spread butter on one side of each slice of bread.
- ➢ Take 2 slices of bread and spread with mayonnaise
- ➢ Mix and top with the chicken,
- ➢ Add tomato, onion, cheese, basil.
- ➢ Cover with remaining bread slices making sure the buttered side up.
- ➢ Place sandwiches on a hot Panini press.
- ➢ Close the Panini press
- ➢ bake for 5 minutes or until golden brown Serve and enjoy

73. CHEESY CHICKEN PANINI

Servings:1　　　　**Cook. Time: 5 Minutes**　　　　**Prep.Time: 10 Minutes**

INGREDIENTS:

- ✓ 2 whole-wheat bread slices
- ✓ 1/4 tsp oregano
- ✓ 2 tbsp marinara sauce
- ✓ 2 1/2 oz chicken breast
- ✓ Cooked & shredded
- ✓ 1/2 cup mozzarella cheese, shredded
- ✓ 1 garlic clove, minced
- ✓ 2 tbsp mushrooms, chopped
- ✓ 2 tbsp onions, chopped
- ✓ 1 tbsp olive oil

DIRECTIONS:

- ➢ Heat the oil in a frying pan over medium heat.
- ➢ Add the garlic, mushrooms and onions,
- ➢ fry until the onion softens.
- ➢ Preheat the Panini press.
- ➢ Take 1 slice of bread
- ➢ Spread with marinara sauce
- ➢ Add chicken, oregano
- ➢ Then sauteed vegetables, cheese.
- ➢ Cover with the remaining slice of bread.
- ➢ Place the sandwich on a hot Panini press.
- ➢ Close Panini press
- ➢ Bake for 5 minutes or until golden brown.

74. RANCH CHICKEN PANINI

Servings:1　　　　**Cook. Time: 5 Minutes**　　　　**Prep.Time: 10 Minutes**

INGREDIENTS

- ✓ 2 bread slices
- ✓ 1 tbsp butter
- ✓ 2 tomato slices
- ✓ 4 bacon slices, cooked
- ✓ 2 Havarti cheese slices
- ✓ 1 cup chicken, cooked and chopped
- ✓ 1/2 cup baby spinach
- ✓ 1 tbsp garlic ranch dressing

DIRECTIONS:

- ➢ Preheat the panini press.
- ➢ Spread butter on one side of each slice of bread.
- ➢ Take 1 slice of bread
- ➢ Spread with garlic ranch sauce
- ➢ Then top with chicken, spinach
- ➢ Add bacon, tomato, cheese.
- ➢ Cover with remaining slice of bread.
- ➢ Make sure the butter side up.
- ➢ Place the sandwich on a hot Panini press.
- ➢ Close the Panini press
- ➢ Bake for 5 minutes or until golden brown.

75. CHICKEN AND HAM PANINI

Servings:4   **Cook. Time: 5 Minutes**   **Prep.Time: 30 Minute**

INGREDIENTS

- ✓ Olive oil
- ✓ 2 hamburger buns
- ✓ If you prefere bread
- ✓ 1 cup Italian dressing
- ✓ 2 chicken breasts
- ✓ 2 slices colby-monterey jack cheese

- ✓ 2 slices monterey jack pepper cheese
- ✓ 4 slices bacon
- ✓ (precooked, 2 per sandwich)
- ✓ 2 slices ham
- ✓ Ranch dressing
- ✓ (Or spicy brown mustard)
- ✓ Banana pepper

DIRECTIONS

- ➢ Marinate the chicken breasts in the Italian seasoning for 30 minutes to an hour.
- ➢ Grill the chicken breasts.

- ➢ Put them on your Panini press
- ➢ or grill forman and give them about 4-5 minutes
- ➢ Alternatively, until the cheese is melted.

To assemble the Panini: Brush olive oil onto your bun, stack the chicken breast, sliced ham, bacon, and cheeses. (If you wish to add the peppers put them on under the cheese). Top with Ranch dressing or spicy brown mustard if you choose.

76. GREEK CHICKEN PANINI

Servings:2   **Cook. Time: 5 Minutes**   **Prep.Time: 10 Minute**

INGREDIENTS:

- ✓ 1 chicken breast, cooked & shredded
- ✓ 4 bread slices
- ✓ 4 oz mozzarella cheese, shredded
- ✓ 1/2 cup roasted red peppers, sliced

- ✓ 2 onion sliced
- ✓ 2 tbsp pesto
- ✓ 1 tbsp butter

DIRECTIONS:

- ➢ Preheat the panini press.
- ➢ Spread butter on one side of each slice of bread.
- ➢ Take 2 slices of bread and spread with pesto.
- ➢ Cover with chicken, onion, red pepper and cheese.
- ➢ Cover with the remaining bread slices.

- ➢ Make sure the buttered side up.
- ➢ Place the sandwiches on a hot Panini press.
- ➢ Close the Panini press
- ➢ Bake for 5 minutes or until golden brown.
- ➢ Serve and enjoy

77. BACON CAESAR AND MOZZARELLA PANINI

Servings:4   **Cook. Time:12 Minutes**   **Prep.Time: 40 Minute**

INGREDIENTS

- ✓ 1 (13 7/8 ounce) can refrigerated pizza crusts
- ✓ 4 teaspoons basil pesto
- ✓ 1/4 cup caesar salad dressing (creamy or vinaigrette style)
- ✓ 8 slices regular mozzarella cheese
- ✓ 1/4 teaspoon fresh ground pepper
- ✓ 12 slices bacon, cooked
- ✓ fresh basil leaf
- ✓ 1/4 cup butter

DIRECTIONS

- ➢ Heat oven to 375°F
- ➢ Spray a large biscuit sheet with nonstick cooking spray.
- ➢ Roll out the pizza crust dough on the biscuit sheet;
- ➢ Press dough into a 16x11-inch rectangle,
- ➢ Gentjy pulling if necessary.
- ➢ Bake 9 to 16 minutes or until light brown.
- ➢ Cool about 15 minutes or until cool enough to handle.
- ➢ Cut the cooled pizza crust in half lengthwise.
- ➢ Crosswise to make 4 rectangles.
- ➢ Remove the rectangles from the baking sheet;
- ➢ Cut each rectangle in half crosswise for a total of 8 squares.
- ➢ On each of the 4 slices of crust, spread 1 teaspoon of pesto and set aside.
- ➢ On each of the remaining 4 slices, spread 1 tbsp Caesar dressing.
- ➢ Place 2 slices of cheese on each slice of crust with Caesar dressing.
- ➢ Top cheese with pepper, 3 slices of bacon, 2 slices of tomato
- ➢ Add 2 basil leaves.
- ➢ Top with remaining crust slices, pesto sides down.
- ➢ Heat a 12-inch skillet or cast-iron frying pan over medium heat until hot.
- ➢ Melt 2 tablespoons of butter in the skillet.
- ➢ Place 2 sandwiches in the skillet.
- ➢ Place a smaller skillet or casserole dish over the buns to flatten them slightly;
- ➢ Hold the pan over the sandwiches while cooking. Cook for 1 to 2 minutes
- ➢ Wait on each side until the bread is golden brown
- ➢ crispy and the fillings are heated through.
- ➢ Remove from pan; cover with foil to keep warm.
- ➢ Repeat with remaining 2 tablespoons butter and rolls

78. BACON RANCH PANINI.

Servings:2   **Cook. Time:5 Minutes**   **Prep.Time: 5 Minute**

INGREDIENTS

- ✓ 4 slices bread
- ✓ 4 tablespoons butter
- ✓ 1 chicken breast
- ✓ 1 tablespoon mustard
- ✓ 4 slices bacon
- ✓ 4 slices cheddar cheese

DIRECTIONS

- ➢ Prepare the bread for the sandwiches
- ➢ Place all the ingredients on one slice of bread
- ➢ Cover with the other slice of bread
- ➢ Toast the sandwich until golden brown
- ➢ Serve when ready

79. CHEDDAR BACON TOMATO PANINI

Servings:4   **Cook. Time:15 Minutes**   **Prep.Time:10 Minute**

INGREDIENTS

- ✓ 8 bread slices
- ✓ 4 tomato slices
- ✓ 8 bacon slices, cooked
- ✓ 10 oz cheddar cheese, shredded
- ✓ 2 tbsp butter, melted

DIRECTIONS

- ➤ Brush butter on one side of each slice of bread.
- ➤ Take 4 slices of bread
- ➤ Sprinkle with 2 tablespoons of cheddar cheese
- ➤ Add the bacon and tomato
- ➤ Sprinkle with the remaining cheese.
- ➤ Cover with the remaining slice of bread.
- ➤ Make sure the buttered side up.
- ➤ Preheat the Panini press.
- ➤ Place 2 sandwiches on hot Panini press.
- ➤ Close the Panini press and bake for 5-6 minutes.
- ➤ Wait until golden brown

80. BACON CHICKEN AVOCADO PANINI

Servings:2   **Cook. Time:5 Minutes**   **Prep.Time:10 Minute**

INGREDIENTS

- ✓ 4 bread slices
- ✓ 6 Provolone cheese slices
- ✓ 1/4 avocado, sliced
- ✓ 1/2 tomato, sliced
- ✓ 2 bacon slices, cooked
- ✓ 1/2 chicken breast, cooked & shredded
- ✓ 1 tbsp butter
- ✓ 1/4 tsp lemon juice
- ✓ 2 tsp hot sauce
- ✓ 1/3 cup mayonnaise
- ✓ Pepper
- ✓ Salt

DIRECTIONS

- ➤ Preheat the panini press.
- ➤ Spread butter on one side of each slice of bread.
- ➤ In a bowl, mix the mayonnaise, hot sauce,
- ➤ add the lemon juice, pepper and salt.
- ➤ Take 2 slices of bread
- ➤ Spread with mayonnaise mixture
- ➤ Cover with chicken, bacon, tomato, avocado, cheese.
- ➤ Cover with remaining bread slices.
- ➤ Make sure the buttered side is on top.
- ➤ Place the sandwiches on a hot Panini press.
- ➤ Close Panini press.
- ➤ Bake for 5 minutes or until golden brown.
- ➤ Serve and enjoy

81. BAT P BACON ARUGULA AND TOMATO PANINI

Servings:1   **Cook. Time:5 Minutes**   **Prep.Time:3 Minute**

INGREDIENTS

- ✓ 2 slices bread (Ciabatta, French, Italian, wheat, sourdough, etc.)
- ✓ 1 teaspoon mayonnaise
- ✓ 2 -3 arugula leaves (a few)
- ✓ 3 slices bacon, fried crisp
- ✓ 1 small roma tomato, sliced thin
- ✓ 1 slice Swiss cheese (or provolone cheese or mozzarella)
- ✓ olive oil

DIRECTIONS

- ➤ Preheat your Panini press/grill.
- ➤ Lightly baste the bread slices on the OUTSIDE with olive oil.
- ➤ Coat the inside of each slice with mayonnaise.
- ➤ Place a slice on the press, oiled side down.
- ➤ On it, make a layer of: rocket, bacon, tomato cheese.
- ➤ Top with the other slice of bread
- ➤ Place the mayonnaise inside the sandwich.
- ➤ Close the press
- ➤ Check the desired degree of cooking in 5 minutes.

82. BACON CHIPOTLE CHICKEN PANINI

Serving: 1   **Prep.Time: 5 Minutes**   **Cook Time 10 Minutes**

INGREDIENTS

- ✓ 2 bread slices
- ✓ 2 tbsp ranch dressing
- ✓ 2 Chipotle gouda cheese slices
- ✓ 2 bacon slices, cooked
- ✓ 1 tomato slice
- ✓ 4 chicken breast slices
- ✓ 2 tsp butter

DIRECTIONS

- ➤ Preheat the panini press.
- ➤ Spread butter on one side of each slice of bread.
- ➤ Take 1 slice of bread
- ➤ Top with chicken slices, tomato, bacon
- ➤ Add cheese and ranch dressing.
- ➤ Cover with remaining slice of bread.
- ➤ Make sure the butter side up.
- ➤ Place the sandwich on a hot Panini press.
- ➤ Close the Panini press and
- ➤ Bake for 5 minutes or until golden brown.

83. BEANS AND BACON PANINI

Servings: 2   **Prep.Time: 5 Minutes**   **Cook Time 5 Minutes**

INGREDIENTS

- ✓ 4 bread slices
- ✓ 4 slices bacon
- ✓ 2 tablespoon barbeque sauce
- ✓ 6-8 oz. baked beans
- ✓ 4 slices cheese

DIRECTIONS

- ➤ Prepare the bread for the sandwiches
- ➤ Place all the ingredients on one slice of bread
- ➤ Cover with the other slice of bread
- ➤ Toast the sandwich until golden brown
- ➤ Serve when ready

84. BACON BISTRO APPLE PANINI

Servings: 6   Prep.Time: 20 Minutes   Cook Time 5 Minutes

INGREDIENTS

- ✓ 12 thick slab bacon, slices cut in half
- ✓ 1 medium apple, thinly sliced
- ✓ 1 tablespoon ginger ale
- ✓ 1 teaspoon lemon juice
- ✓ 1/4 cup apple jelly
- ✓ 4 teaspoons minced fresh tarragon
- ✓ 12 slices sourdough bread
- ✓ 6 slices reduced-fat havarti cheese
- ✓ 2 tablespoons Dijon mustard
- ✓ 3 tablespoons butter, softened

DIRECTIONS

- ➤ In a large frying pan, cook bacon over medium heat until crispy.
- ➤ Remove to paper towels to drain.
- ➤ In a small bowl, mix apple with ginger ale and lemon juice; set aside.
- ➤ Place gelatin in a small microwave-safe bowl;
- ➤ Microwave on high for 20-30 seconds or until softened.
- ➤ Stir in tarragon.
- ➤ Spread gelatin mixture on six slices of bread.
- ➤ Top with cheese, apple, bacon.
- ➤ Spread mustard on remaining bread;
- ➤ Place bacon on top.
- ➤ Spread outer sides of sandwiches with butter.
- ➤ Bake on a Panini machine or indoor grill for 3-4 minutes
- ➤ (or until the bread is golden brown and the cheese is melted).

85. BREAKFAST ON THE GO BACON PANINI

Servings : 2   Prep.Time: 4 Minutes   Cook Time:20 Minutes

INGREDIENTS

- ✓ 4 slices Canadian bacon
- ✓ 2 teaspoons butter
- ✓ 2 eggs
- ✓ salt
- ✓ fresh ground black pepper
- ✓ 2 English muffins, split
- ✓ 1 tablespoon butter, melted
- ✓ 2 ounces cheddar cheese, sliced

DIRECTIONS

- ➤ Preheat the Panini grill to a high temperature.
- ➤ Place the bacon on the bottom plate of the Panini grill,
- ➤ Close the top plate
- ➤ Grill until crispy, 1-2 minutes.
- ➤ Remove and set aside; clean grill plates.
- ➤ In a nonstick skillet, melt 2 t butter over medium heat.
- ➤ Crack eggs into the pan.
- ➤ Cook until whites are set but yolks are still runny.
- ➤ Season with salt and pepper.
- ➤ Turn eggs with a rubber spatula
- ➤ Cook until yolks are set; remove from heat.
- ➤ Place muffins, cut side down on a work surface
- ➤ Brush the crusts with melted butter.
- ➤ Turn the muffins over
- ➤ On bottom half of each muffin, layer evenly with bacon
- ➤ Add, cheese and also the egg
- ➤ Cover with the top halves and press down gently to pack.
- ➤ Place sandwiches in grill, close top plate
- ➤ Bake until golden brown, 3-4 minutes.
- ➤ Serve immediately

86. BACON TURKEY BURGERS

Servings: 5   **Prep.Time: 8 Minutes**   **Cook Time:10 Minutes**

INGREDIENTS
- ✓ 1 lb ground turkey
- ✓ 1/2 tsp garlic powder
- ✓ 1/3 cup bacon, chopped
- ✓ 1/3 cup green onions, chopped
- ✓ 1 cup cheddar cheese, shredded
- ✓ 1/4 cup BBQ sauce
- ✓ Pepper
- ✓ Salt

DIRECTIONS
- ➢ Preheat the panini press.
- ➢ Add all the ingredients to the mixing bowl and mix until well combined.
- ➢ Make 5 patties from the mixture and spray with cooking spray.
- ➢ Place the patties on the hot Panini press and cook for 4 minutes on each side.
- ➢ Serve and enjoy

87. BRIE CRANBERRY AND BACON PANINI

Servings:2   **Cook. Time:10 Minutes**   **Prep.Time:5 Minute**

INGREDIENTS
- ✓ 4 slices bread (I use 2 Panini rolls but any bread will do)
- ✓ 4 slices brie cheese, 2 for each sandwich
- ✓ 5 tablespoons cranberry sauce
- ✓ 4 slices streaky bacon, cooked
- ✓ butter, if using regular bread

DIRECTIONS
- ➢ If using sandwiches, cut each sandwich in half.
- ➢ If using normal bread, spread the outside of each slice.
- ➢ Add the butter.
- ➢ Spread 2 1/2 tablespoons of the cranberry sauce
- ➢ the sauce should be on each on 2 slices of bread.
- ➢ Layer the brie on top of the blueberry sauce.
- ➢ Top with 2 slices of bacon after the top layer of bread.
- ➢ Remembering to keep the buttered side facing out.
- ➢ Use a wire rack to cook the sandwiches.
- ➢ Press the lid down to heat the sandwich.
- ➢ Cook for a few minutes until the cheese has melted.
- ➢ Alternatively, cook in a frying pan,
- ➢ Then press the sandwich firmly down with a spatula while cooking.
  Serve hot

88. BACON BISCUIT PANINI

Servings:2   **Cook. Time:5 Minutes**   **Prep.Time:5 Minute**

INGREDIENTS
- ✓ 2 fried eggs
- ✓ 2 slices bacon
- ✓ 2 biscuits
- ✓ 2 cheese slices
- ✓ 2 bread slices

DIRECTIONS
- ➢ Prepare the bread for the sandwiches
- ➢ Place all the ingredients on one slice of bread
- ➢ Cover with the other slice of bread
- ➢ Toast the sandwich until golden brown
- ➢ Serve when ready

89. AMERICAN ROAST BEEF PANINI

Servings:2   **Cook. Time:5 Minutes**   **Prep.Time:30 Minute**

INGREDIENTS

- ✓ 3 tablespoons mayonnaise
- ✓ 1 tablespoon sour cream
- ✓ 1 tablespoon prepared horseradish
- ✓ 1 tablespoon chopped fresh marjoram
- ✓ 4 slices whole-wheat country bread
- ✓ (or 2 ciabatta panini rolls, split or 4 slices rye bread
- ✓ (Alternatively 2 ciabatta sandwich rolls, split)

- ✓ 1 tablespoon unsalted butter, at room temperature
- ✓ 1/2 lb roast beef, thinly sliced
- ✓ salt
- ✓ fresh ground black pepper
- ✓ 1 ounce parmesan cheese, shaved with a vegetable peeler
- ✓ watercress, 1 small bunch, tough stems removed

DIRECTIONS

- ➢ In a small bowl, mix together the mayonnaise, sour cream, horseradish and marjoram;
- ➢ Let stand for about 10 minutes at room temperature to allow the flavours to meld.
- ➢ (alternatively, cover and refrigerate for up to 6 hours.
- ➢ (if refrigerated, bring back to room temperature before use).
- ➢ Preheat the sandwich griddle.
- ➢ Place the bread slices, cut sides down, on a work surface.
- ➢ Spread 1 side of each slice of bread with butter.
- ➢ Turn and spread the unbuttered sides of the bread with the mayonnaise mixture.

- ➢ On each of the 2 slices of bread, with the mayonnaise mixture on top, place half of the roast beef.
- ➢ Season generously with salt and pepper.
- ➢ Divide the cheese and watercress over the top.
- ➢ Cover with the remaining 2 slices of bread, mayonnaise sides down,
- ➢ Press down gently to pack.
- ➢ Place the Panini on the grill,
- ➢ Close the top plate,
- ➢ Cook until the bread is golden brown and the
- ➢ toasted, the meat is heated through and the watercress is almost wilted,
- ➢ Cooking time 3-5 minutes.
- ➢ Cut each sandwich in half diagonally.
- ➢ Serve immediately.

90. MEDITERRANEAN PANINI

Servings:2   **Cook. Time:5 Minutes**   **Prep.Time:5 Minute**

INGREDIENTS

- ✓ 4 bread slices
- ✓ 1 zucchini
- ✓ 4 slices cheese

- ✓ ½ cup red peppers
- ✓ ¼ cup basil leaves

DIRECTIONS

- ➢ Prepare the bread for the sandwiches
- ➢ Place all the ingredients on one slice of bread
- ➢ Cover with the other slice of bread

- ➢ Toast the sandwich until golden brown
- ➢ Serve when ready

91. ITALIAN SUN-DRIED TOMATO SPINACH PANINI

Servings:2   **Cook. Time:5 Minutes**   **Prep.Time:10 Minute**

INGREDIENTS

- 4 bread slices
- 1/4 cup parmesan cheese, shaved
- 1/4 cup sun-dried tomatoes, sliced
- 1 cup baby spinach
- 1 tbsp butter
- 1/4 tsp Italian seasoning
- 1/4 cup ricotta cheese
- 1/4 cup goat cheese

DIRECTIONS

- Preheat the bread press.
- Spread butter on one side of each slice of bread.
- In a small bowl, mix the ricotta cheese and Italian dressing,
- Add the goat cheese.
- Take 2 slices of bread
- Spread with the cheese mixture
- Cover with spinach, tomatoes and Parmesan cheese.
- Cover with the remaining bread slices.
- Make sure the buttered side up.
- Place the sandwich in a hot press.
- Close the sandwich press.
- Bake for 5 minutes or until golden brown.
- Serve and enjoy.

92. ITALIAN GARLIC BREAD BRUSCHETTA

Servings:8   **Cook. Time:10 Minutes**   **Prep.Time:10 Minute**

INGREDIENTS

- 8 Italian bread slices
- 1 garlic clove, minced
- 1/4 cup olive oil
- For salad:
- 1 tbsp balsamic vinegar
- 1 tbsp olive oil
- 2 garlic cloves, minced
- 1/4 cup basil, sliced
- 1/4 cup parmesan cheese, grated
- 2 cups cherry tomatoes, diced
- Pepper
- Salt

DIRECTIONS

- Preheat the Panini press.
- In a small bowl, mix the olive oil and garlic.
- Brush the bread slices with the oil and place on a hot Panini press. In batches.
- Close the Panini press and bake for 8-10 minutes.
- Wait until golden brown.
- In a bowl, mix all the salad ingredients.
- Divide the salad over the toasted bread slices.
- Serve.
-

93. AMERICAN BREAKFAST PANINI

Servings:2   **Cook. Time:4 Minutes**   **Prep.Time:5 Minute**

INGREDIENTS

- 1 (12 inch) hoagie rolls (or bread of your choice)
- 2 slices yellow American cheese
- 4 slices deli ham
- 4 slices sweet roasted peppers

DIRECTIONS

- Prepare the bread for the sandwiches
- Place all the ingredients on one slice of bread
- Cover with the other slice of bread
- Toast the sandwich until golden brown
- Serve when ready

94. VIETNAM'S BÁNH MÌ

Servings:2   **Cook. Time:5 Minutes**   **Prep.Time:70 Minute**

INGREDIENTS

PICKLES:
- ✓ 1/2 cup rice vinegar
- ✓ 1/3 cup granulated sugar
- ✓ 1/3 cup water

PANINI:
- ✓ 6 (2-ounce) boneless pork breakfast cutlets
- ✓ 1/4 teaspoon kosher salt
- ✓ Cooking spray
- ✓ 1 (12-ounce) French bread baguette (16 inches long)

- ✓ 2 teaspoons sambal oelek
- ✓ 1/2 cup shredded carrot
- ✓ 1/3 cup matchstick-cut radishes
- ✓ 1/3 cup thinly sliced red onion

- ✓ 1/4 cup light mayonnaise
- ✓ 1 teaspoon sambal oelek
- ✓ 1/4 cup thinly sliced peeled cucumber
- ✓ 1/2 cup cilantro leaves

DIRECTIONS

- ➢ To prepare the pickles, combine the first 4 ingredients
- ➢ (through the sambal oelek) in a small saucepan.
- ➢ Bring to the boil, stirring until the sugar dissolves.
- ➢ Remove from heat.
- ➢ Add carrot, radish, onion.
- ➢ Let stand, uncovered, at room temperature 1 hour.
- ➢ Preheat grill.
- ➢ Place pork between 2 sheets of cling film;
- ➢ Pound thickness to 1/8 inch.
- ➢ Use a meat tenderizer or small heavy skillet.
- ➢ Sprinkle pork evenly with salt,
- ➢ Place on broiler pan coated with cooking spray.
- ➢ Broil 5 minutes. Remove from pan.
- ➢ Cut bread in half lengthwise.
- ➢ Hollow out bottom half of bread, leaving a 1/2-inch
- ➢ thick shell;
- ➢ Reserve torn bread for another use.
- ➢ Place bread halves, cut sides up, on a baking sheet.
- ➢ Broil 1 minute or until toasted.
- ➢ Combine mayo.1 teaspoon sambal oelek in a small bowl.
- ➢ Spread mayonnaise mixture on cut side of top of bread.
- ➢ Layer pickled vegetables, pork slices, cucumber
- ➢ Add the cilantro evenly to the bottom of the bread.
- ➢ Cover with the top of the bread.
- ➢ Cut the sandwich into 4 equal portions.

95. FRENCH LEMON AVOCADO BRUSCHETTA

Servings:8   **Cook. Time:10 Minutes**   **Prep.Time:10 Minute**

INGREDIENTS

- ✓ 8 French bread slices
- ✓ 2 tbsp olive oil
- ✓ For topping:
- ✓ 8 Roma tomatoes, diced
- ✓ 1 tsp olive oil
- ✓ 1 tbsp balsamic vinegar
- ✓ 2 garlic cloves, minced
- ✓ 1/3 cup basil, chopped
- ✓ 1/2 tsp lemon juice
- ✓ 3 avocados, diced
- ✓ 1/4 tsp salt

DIRECTIONS

- ➢ Preheat the Panini press.
- ➢ Brush the bread slices with oil and place them on the hot Panini press. In batches.
- ➢ Close the Panini press and bake for 8-10 minutes.
- ➢ Wait until they are golden brown.
- ➢ In a bowl, add all the seasoning ingredients and mix well.
- ➢ Spread the seasoning mixture over the toasted bread slices.
- ➢ Serve

96. FRANCH PANERA CHOCOLATE PANINI

Serving:1   **Cook. Time:10 Minutes**   **Prep.Time:5 Minute**

INGREDIENTS

- ✓ 2 slices of panera ciabatta or 2 slices French bread
- ✓ 1 ounce premium bittersweet chocolate

DIRECTIONS

- ➢ The chocolate used varies according to the type of bread used.
- ➢ Cover a piece of bread with about 3/8 inch of chocolate.
- ➢ Place the chocolate on a slice of bread,
- ➢ Spread evenly and up to 1/2 inch from all edges.
- ➢ Leave room for the chocolate to melt.
- ➢ Cover with the other slice of bread.
- ➢ Toast on a grill or in an oven at 500° F for 5 minutes.
- ➢ Turn the sandwich to avoid being burnt.
- ➢ Remove from oven when both sides are lightly toasted.
- ➢ Check that the chocolate is melting
- ➢ Cool briefly before serving.
- ➢ The chocolate will be very hot
- ➢ Pat carefully when panini comes out
- ➢ Make sure to cool a little while

97. CHINESE STEAK PANINI

Servings:2   **Cook. Time:5 Minutes**   **Prep.Time:5 Minute**

INGREDIENTS

- ✓ 4 bread slices
- ✓ 2 rib eye steaks
- ✓ 4 fried eggs
- ✓ 1 tablespoon parsley
- ✓ 4 tablespoons butter
- ✓ 4 slices cheddar cheese

DIRECTIONS

- ➢ Prepare the bread for the sandwiches
- ➢ Place all the ingredients on one slice of bread
- ➢ Cover with the other slice of bread
- ➢
- ➢ Toast the sandwich until golden brown
- ➢ Serve when ready

98. CHINESE ROAST PORK PANINI

Serving:1   Cook. Time:10 Minutes   Prep.Time:5 Minute

INGREDIENTS
- ✓ 1 (12 -16 ounce) pork tenderloin, trimmed
- ✓ cut crosswise into 2 large pieces
- ✓ salt and pepper
- ✓ 2 tablespoons vegetable oil
- ✓ 1 onion, chopped
- ✓ 2 tablespoons hoisin sauce
- ✓ 2 tablespoons honey
- ✓ 1 tablespoon sesame oil
- ✓ 1 tablespoon soy sauce
- ✓ 4 -6 challah rolls, split (3 to 4 inches wide)

DIRECTIONS
- ➤ Preheat the oven to 450°F.
- ➤ Season the pork with salt and pepper.
- ➤ Heat a heavy, medium oven
- ➤ Place a skillet over medium-high heat.
- ➤ Add 1 tablespoon oil, then the pork;
- ➤ Cook, turning, until golden brown, about 2 minutes.
- ➤ Transfer to oven and roast
- ➤ Wait until a thermometer registers 150,
- ➤ Time about 10 minutes.
- ➤ Transfer to a cutting board
- ➤ Allow to rest for 10 minutes
- ➤ Cut into 1/2 inch cubes.
- ➤ In a small frying pan, heat 1 tablespoon oil.
- ➤ Heat over medium heat.
- ➤ Add onion
- ➤ Cook, stirring, until softened, about 8 minutes.
- ➤ Take a large bowl,
- ➤ whisk together the hoisin sauce, honey,
- ➤ Add the sesame oil and soy sauce.
- ➤ Stir in the onion and pork and its juices.
- ➤ Preheat a Panini press.
- ➤ Divide the pork mixture evenly between the rolls.
- ➤ Then cover with the tops.
- ➤ Working in batches
- ➤ if necessary, grill until golden brown and crispy

99. CHINESE CAULIFLOWER CURRY PANINI

Servings:2   Cook. Time:5 Minutes   Prep.Time:5 Minute

INGREDIENTS
- ✓ 2 tsp tamarind paste
- ✓ ¼ cup roasted cauliflower
- ✓ 3-4 slices roasted potato
- ✓ 1 tsp curry powder
- ✓ ¼ tsp turmeric
- ✓ ¼ cup peas
- ✓ 8 oz. chickpeas
- ✓ 4 bread slices

DIRECTIONS
- ➤ Prepare the bread for the sandwiches
- ➤ Place all the ingredients on one slice of bread
- ➤ Cover with the other slice of bread
- ➤ Toast the sandwich until golden brown.

100. SIMPLE PANINI PROSCIUTTO

Servings:2   Cook. Time:5 Minutes   Prep.Time:5 Minute

INGREDIENTS
- ✓ 4 bread slices
- ✓ ¼ tsp black pepper
- ✓ 8 oz. prosciutto
- ✓ 8 oz. swiss cheese
- ✓ 2 fried eggs

DIRECTIONS
- ➤ Prepare the bread for the sandwiches
- ➤ Place all the ingredients on one slice of bread
- ➤ Cover with the other slice of bread
- ➤ Toast the sandwich until golden brown
- ➤ Serve when ready

101. DELICIOUS EGG PROSCIUTTO PANINI

Servings:4   **Cook. Time:15 Minutes**   **Prep.Time:10 Minute**

INGREDIENTS

- ✓ 3 eggs
- ✓ 2 egg whites
- ✓ 8 tsp butter, melted
- ✓ 1/2 cup cheddar cheese, shredded
- ✓ 8 prosciutto slices
- ✓ 8 bread slices
- ✓ 1 tbsp maple syrup
- ✓ 1 tbsp Dijon mustard
- ✓ 6 tbsp milk

DIRECTIONS

- ➢ In a small bowl, beat the eggs and milk,
- ➢ Add the egg whites.
- ➢ Spray the pan with cooking spray.
- ➢ Heat over medium heat.
- ➢ Pour eggs into hot pan
- ➢ Cook until set.
- ➢ Then mix the ingredients.
- ➢ Brush butter on one side of each slice of bread.
- ➢ Stir in maple syrup and mustard.
- ➢ Add the spread on 4 slices of bread
- ➢ Then top with the scrambled egg, ham and cheese.
- ➢ Cover with the remaining slice of bread.
- ➢ Make sure the buttered side up.
- ➢ Preheat the Panini press.
- ➢ Place 2 sandwiches on hot press.
- ➢ Close Panini press, bake for 3-4 minutes.
- ➢ Wait until golden brown.

102. PROSCIUTTO AND FONTINA PANINI

Servings:4   **Cook. Time:15 Minutes**   **Prep.Time:10 Minute**

INGREDIENTS

- ✓ 1 (5 1/4 ounce) package focaccia bread
- ✓ 8 slices prosciutto (about 2 ounces)
- ✓ 1/4 cup shredded Fontina cheese
- ✓ 1 cup trimmed arugula or 1 cup watercress
- ✓ 2 red onions, slices separated into rings (1/8-inch-thick)
- ✓ 2 teaspoons balsamic vinegar
- ✓ 1/8 teaspoon pepper

DIRECTIONS

- ➢ Cut each slice of bread in half horizontally.
- ➢ Divide the slices of ham between the lower halves of the bread.
- ➢ Cover each half of the bread with fontina cheese and rocket.
- ➢ Add the red onion slices.
- ➢ Pour the balsamic vinegar over the bread.
- ➢ Sprinkle with pepper;
- ➢ Cover with the top half of the bread
- ➢ Wrap the sandwiches tightly in aluminium foil,
- ➢ Then bake at 300° for 15 minutes.

103. PESTO PROSCIUTTO PANINI

Servings:2   **Cook. Time:5 Minutes**   **Prep.Time:10 Minute**

INGREDIENTS

- ✓ 4 bread slices
- ✓ 1/4 lb provolone cheese, sliced
- ✓ 1/4 lb prosciutto, sliced
- ✓ 1 cup baby spinach
- ✓ 2 tbsp pesto
- ✓ 2 tbsp mayonnaise
- ✓ 1 tbsp butter

DIRECTIONS

- ➤ Preheat the Panini press.
- ➤ In a small bowl, mayonnaise, pesto.
- ➤ Spread butter on one side of each slice of bread.
- ➤ Take 2 slices of bread and spread with mayonnaise.
- ➤ Cover with ham, spinach and cheese.
- ➤ Cover with the remaining slices of bread.
- ➤ Make sure the buttered side up.
- ➤ Place the sandwiches on a hot press.
- ➤ Close the sandwich press and
- ➤ Bake for 5 minutes
- ➤ Wait until golden brown

104. ARTICHOKE AND PROSCIUTTO PANINI

Servings:4   **Cook. Time:3 Minutes**   **Prep.Time:2 Minutes**

INGREDIENTS

- ✓ 4 ciabatta rolls or 4 (6 inch) baguette, halved lengthwise
- ✓ 1/4 cup extra virgin olive oil
- ✓ salt & freshly ground black pepper

- ✓ 1/2 lb sliced prosciutto
  - ✓ 1 jar artichoke hearts, drained
  - ✓ flattened slightly
  - ✓ 8 arugula leaves

DIRECTIONS

- ➤ Brush the cut sides of the ciabatta with olive oil.
- ➤ Season with salt and pepper.
- ➤ Layer the ham, artichoke hearts and rocket
- ➤ And rocket on the ciabatta.
- ➤ Close the panini.
- ➤ Set a large cast-iron pan
- ➤ (Or a griddle on a moderately high heat).

- ➤ Arrange the Panini in the pan
- ➤ Weight them down with a smaller pan.
- ➤ Cook the Panini until the outside is crispy.
- ➤ Wait for the filling to heat through,
- ➤ Cook 3 minutes per side.
- ➤ Cut the Panini in half and serve immediately

105.   PROSCIUTTO AND SMOKED GOUDA PANINI

Servings:10   **Cook. Time:5 Minutes**   **Prep.Time:10 Minutes**

INGREDIENTS
- ✓ 20 (1-ounce) slices Italian bread
- ✓ Cooking spray
- ✓ 6 ounces smoked Gouda cheese, thinly sliced
- ✓ 6 ounces thinly sliced prosciutto

DIRECTIONS
- ➤ Coat 1 side of each slice of bread with cooking spray.
- ➤ Place 10 slices of bread,
- ➤ place the coated sides down, on a work surface.
- ➤ Divide the cheese and ham
- ➤ evenly between 10 slices of bread.
- ➤ Cover with the remaining slices of bread
- ➤ Cover them with the sides facing upwards.
- ➤ Heat a large non-stick frying pan over a medium heat.
- ➤ Cook the sandwiches 5 minutes
- ➤ (on each side or until lightly browned).
- ➤ Wait for the cheese to melt,
- ➤ Press down with a spatula to flatten

106.   PROVOLONE PROSCIUTTO PANINI

Servings:4   **Cook. Time:10 Minutes**   **Prep.Time:10 Minutes**

INGREDIENTS
- ✓ 8 bread slices
- ✓ 8 oz prosciutto slices
- ✓ 12 provolone cheese slices
- ✓ 2 tbsp butter
- ✓ 2 tsp rosemary, chopped
- ✓ 2 red bell peppers, cut into strips

DIRECTIONS
- ➤ Preheat the panini press.
- ➤ Spread butter on one side of each slice of bread.
- ➤ Take 4 slices of bread and
- ➤ Top with ham, rosemary,
- ➤ Add the peppers and cheese.
- ➤ Cover with the remaining bread slices.
- ➤ Make sure the buttered side is on top.
- ➤ Place 2 sandwiches on a hot press.
- ➤ Close the press and
- ➤ Bake for 5 minutes
- ➤ (Or until golden brown).
- ➤ Serve and enjoy

107.   DELICIOUS PROSCIUTTO SERRANO PANINI

Servings:4   **Cook. Time:10 Minutes**   **Prep.Time:10 Minutes**

INGREDIENTS
- ✓ 2 bread slices
- ✓ 1 tbsp butter
- ✓ 1 tsp Dijon mustard
- ✓ 2 Serrano Prosciutto ham slices
- ✓ 2 provolone cheese slices

DIRECTIONS
- ➤ Preheat the panini press.
- ➤ Spread butter on one side of each slice of bread.
- ➤ Take 1 slice of bread
- ➤ Spread with mustard
- ➤ Cover with ham and cheese.
- ➤ Cover with the remaining slice of bread.
- ➤ Make sure the butter side is on top.
- ➤ Place the sandwiches on a hot press.
- ➤ Close the sandwich press.
- ➤ Bake for 5 minutes
- ➤ (or until golden brown).
- ➤ Serve and enjoy.

Thanks for reading this book

CPSIA information can be obtained
at www.ICGtesting.com
Printed in the USA
BVHW060124180521
607551BV00011B/1205